Information, The Hidden Side of Life

"In the beginning was the Word..."

John 1:1
New International Version

Series Editor
Jean-Charles Pomerol

Information,
The Hidden Side of Life

Cédric Gaucherel
Pierre-Henri Gouyon
Jean-Louis Dessalles

WILEY

First published 2019 in Great Britain and the United States by ISTE Ltd and John Wiley & Sons, Inc.

ISTE Ltd
27-37 St George's Road
London SW19 4EU
UK

www.iste.co.uk

John Wiley & Sons, Inc.
111 River Street
Hoboken, NJ 07030
USA

www.wiley.com

The rights of Cédric Gaucherel, Pierre-Henri Gouyon and Jean-Louis Dessalles to be identified as the authors of this work have been asserted by them in accordance with the Copyright, Designs and Patents Act 1988.

Library of Congress Control Number: 2018960339

British Library Cataloguing-in-Publication Data
A CIP record for this book is available from the British Library
ISBN 978-1-78630-424-7

Contents

Preface

"The reader of this sentence will cease to
exist when he has finished reading."
Metamagical Themas, Douglas Hofstadter

This book grew out of a meeting that brought together three scientists, who had different backgrounds, and who worked in different disciplines, but who all had this in common: their activities had to do with the living entity. Confronting each of them in their own way was the question: *what is information?*

Whether in ecosystems, human language, genetics or evolution of living organisms, one comes face to face with the idea that information forms the substance of the system(s) being studied, then reproduced, transmitted, coded and decoded, or manipulated in other ways. Such information may not be equally important to everyone, it may not be carried by the same channel, or perhaps even be of the same nature. Yet, one cannot afford to overlook the importance of the concept while continuing to speak of it without a proper understanding of what the much-used term means. The information that we exchange and talk about every day is coded in our language. Now, are other languages coded differently, say nature's languages? Can we define them, analyze them and quantify them?

Quite possibly, part of what we are going to say here may appear obvious to some readers, but unacceptable to others. Considering the gap between these two reactions, however, it is reassuring that we come across both kinds of comment, perhaps in a sign that there is something non-consensual behind seemingly mundane ideas. Now, we are not quite done with this theme yet, and, in fact, this is going to open up further vistas of thinking. We hope that the publication of this essay will make possible an elaboration of the issue, and lead to fruitful discussions with those who find these questions interesting.

One difficulty that appears immediately pertinent has to do with the very nature of information. Is it material or is it not? The answer: while the channels used in transmitting it are material, information itself is not material.

Well, this is only the first of our difficulties. Our science does not readily accept non-material entities. Let us not forget that the absence of materiality was a major argument in the rejection of Newton's theory: the force of gravity appeared quite esoteric, since the force is acting at a distance, without material support. In contrast, the solar turbulences mentioned by Descartes appeared to be much more real or tangible. Yet, while following the same Aristotelian line of thinking, up to the end of the 18th Century, it seemed reasonable to consider fire an *element*, to the point of giving it a name: phlogiston. A process received the status of matter through a distortion of reality. It was left to the times of Lavoisier to demonstrate the difference between a material entity and a chemical reaction, and thereby to bring to an end a misconception that had persisted for over 2,000 years.

Let us rid ourselves of this obsessive habit of seeing everything in terms of matter. Information, even though carried by material agents, is nevertheless different from them. Now, how can a non-material entity act on matter? While trying to resolve this apparent paradox, we need to remember that, while information is certainly non-material, it is active across channels of communication, themselves material.

Does not Léo Ferré, in his *Il n'y a plus rien* ("There's Nothing Any More"), praise the non-material virtues of information?

"Peddle your ideas like drugs… You risk nothing at the borders. Nothing in your hands, nothing in your pockets, it's all there in your head!

'Anything to declare?'

'Nothing!'

'What is your name?'

'Karl Marx.'

'All right. Move on!'"

Indeed, Karl Marx probably produced nothing other than information. He bore no arms, raised no army. For all that, for this generation of ours, having lived in a world split into two blocs, through nuclear horror and the wars that raged from Vietnam to Nicaragua and Cuba and Afghanistan, and that reshaped (and continue to reshape) the geopolitical environment, how materially influential this information of Marx's has been.

While we (the three scientists) were still getting to know one another, one of us expressed to Jean-Marc Levy-Leblond his desire to work on the concept of information. "Is that a concept?" he had asked. Indeed, information is not yet a concept. Could we build one out of it?

Cédric GAUCHEREL
Pierre-Henri GOUYON
Jean-Louis DESSALES
October 2018

Introduction

Dear reader, do you know that an extraordinary happening is taking place at this very moment? Your eyes are taking in a linear message in a to-and-fro movement, line by line. The characters that make up the message are imprinting themselves on your retina, because of the sophisticated optical system that you possess. The retinal cells convert the stimuli into an impulse that then enters the brain. That organ then interprets the signal, and ... , well, the information that the text had embodied has now entered your mind! Now, dear reader, would you please turn the page?

Thank you. Now, did you notice that something incredible just happened? A piece of information, non-material, was carried by a means, which itself was material (we will say more about this a little later), as described above, and produced a result which was physical. You moved your finger, and turned the page! The physical was put through a change by the action of a piece of non-physical information. That is the sort of thing we are used to. Indeed, our body is a kind of machine that converts information into action. Certain types of information, such as the recipes you find in cookery books, are clearly meant for use with material things.

This work will attempt to consider whatever could be treated as information from the point of view of science. Our times appear to be very much under the influence of that entity. One might ask if this information-age society of ours is seriously looking into what it is that it is talking so much about. The sciences speak about it. Physics and mathematics have developed a now-classical theory of information. As we will see shortly, these disciplines have only captured a fragment of the idea that we have developed in this presentation. Biology has been advancing increasingly with the study of genetics and epigenetics. Ecology takes account of information relating to different levels of organizations, individuals and communities of species. Information underpins new and emerging fields of study such as communication science and technology. Linguistics and the different branches of the humanities also speak of information, which lies at the heart of the network of relationships. Now, what *is* information about?

It seems advisable at this point to try to disambiguate the term "information", this notional entity that reproduces itself, transforms itself, elaborates itself and expresses itself ... There are to be found in history and the philosophy of science concepts that are both central and indefinable, such as time, which can be measured but not defined. On the other hand, we have an instinctive perception of what time is. Saint Augustine wrote around the year 400: "What is time? If I am not asked the time, I know it; but, if I wish to explain it, I don't know it! And, yet – and I say this with all confidence – I know that if nothing happened, there would have been no past; if nothing is going to happen, there would be no future; and if nothing existed, there would be no present". Right or wrong, we have the feeling that we know what time is about, and we are compelled to adapt our definition to particular needs.

It is much the same for the notion of information. Rather than look for a definition, should we not content ourselves with stating its characteristics, and search for a measure that will serve to identify it? The communications specialist studies the movement of information. The linguist studies how information is coded in languages, and how such codes evolve. The biologist investigates how genetic information interacts with the environment so as to ensure the production of an organism. The geneticist examines the transmission of genetic information, while the evolutionist devotes attention to learning how genetic information progressively led to the creation of widely differing organisms. What interests the ethologist is how information travels among a group of living beings. The ecologist quantifies the information contained in the diversity of a community of species, or within the spatial distribution of the components of an ecosystem. The science of nature constantly encounters this notion of information while dispensing with a definition of the term.

To return to our example – this book contains information. Strictly speaking, the information is not non-material in that a material entity is carrying it. However, in a certain sense, the material nature of that entity is unimportant. That material might be paper, or magnetic tape, a USB key, a CD, a hard disk, etc. If you were to read the text aloud to someone else, it would be the vibrations of air that would carry the information. If you were to learn the contents by heart, then your cerebral neurons would store it by a yet-unknown method. In none of these ways would the information be reducible to the material that carried it; the two entities are clearly different. Imagine that someone asks you for your impression of the novel you last read. You might answer somewhat like this: "It had a red cover, and had 250 pages of 100-gram grained vellum, with black-and-white printing". This is what could happen if you confuse information and its material medium.

Information, which is carried by a material medium, and from which, however, it differs, possesses some remarkable characteristics. For one thing, it can be transferred from one sort of medium to another while remaining more or less unchanged, though not under all conditions. For another, it can be done into several copies or versions. Yet again, it can act on matter, as we have seen above. What a funny entity, what a funny concept!

I.1. We can change the medium without changing the information

Copy a text, photocopy it, scan it, photograph it, print it, read it, memorize it, etc., there are so many ways of transferring information from one medium to another. Some of these methods are rather good at making copies of data that will be close to the original, but to be able to do this you would need certain special kinds of medium. Other methods permit the data to be expressed, though necessitating a change in form.

Making identical copies seems simple enough. Just copy the stuff – as simple as that...or almost! Mind the *almost*. The fact is that we can show with the help of thermodynamics that it is impossible to make a *perfect* copy of a given message without a single error, within a reasonable amount of time and with limited resources. In other words, a copy is bound to differ from the original message, given the constraints mentioned. If I were only to change a single symbol in a novel, say by turning it into bold, the novel would remain the same, except when, through sheer happenstance, the changed symbol could have meant a total change in the narration. We can imagine a story like that, but it is not going to be easy. A copy of a copy of a copy of a copy ... would you have a copy at some point that does not differ from the original? There is this game in which one individual tells a story to the next one, and the last version turns out to be wholly different from the first one.[1] We shall see that evolution and the dynamics of evolution work this way in biology and, equally, in evolution. Now, when is one to say that the information is no longer the same? Is not that when it becomes possible to quantify the difference between the original and the copy?

We may wish to express a particular piece of information by moving it into another medium. For instance, when I read a printed text, the information passes from paper onto my brain. A major modification has taken place here. My brain has become the interpreter. That said, it must be

---

1 There are instances in which such changes do not occur. Rumors have been known to remain astonishingly unchanged over countless narrations. Some see in this phenomenon a hint that some elements of information, known as memes, lend themselves to propagation in their entirety (Chapter 1). A well-known example is the story of the woman who used to dry her dog in an oven, with its heat turned very low, and who later tried to do the same thing with her new microwave. This story has remained unchanged as it traveled through different countries – the United States, Great Britain and France – to the best of our knowledge.

added that I may change, to some degree, the information that was delivered by the text I read and learnt by heart so that I might remember it. Did we say *to some degree?* That implies a quantitative variation. Is there a value hidden behind this idea? If we were to ask a philosopher or a linguist if it is possible to measure the information content of a text, their first reaction might be to say that such a thing would not be possible. We shall return to this point in Chapter 4. Most would agree, in this context, that a given text suffers a loss in translation. Now, how on earth could one speak of *loss* if there were not a notion of quantity in the first place?

The problem arises especially from the fact that a transfer of information, such as that of text printed on paper being moved onto my brain, is more than just a transfer. An action such as this underpins the very existence of the particular information. If I were to open a book that contained signs I did not understand, I would not receive the information that the printed text carried. Printed text only carries information if I am able to understand that text, if I am able to make sense of that text, if that text is capable of action on a form of matter. What now?

I.2. Where does information exist?

When all is said and done, the information the novel contained, or the information the recipe book contained, does not exist only on the paper on which it was printed. It did not exist in my brain until I read the text. It was necessarily the result of an interaction between the two. It is an undeniable fact that I cannot define a piece of information independently of the system for which it is meant. Did I say *meant?* Is it always the case that every piece of information should be meant for a receiver? Certainly not!

When I see the sun rising, I know roughly what time it is and, again roughly, my direction. The information the sunrise conveyed was not meant for me. In fact, there would have been no information in that event if I had not interpreted the sunrise the way I did. The event would have taken place even if no one interpreted it, but it would not have contained the particular information. Of course, this would not have been the case with the printed text, which would not have come into being if no one were able to interpret it. Here information has been the result of the way in which I interpreted what I perceived in the environment. The environment contained information since there was in existence a reading system, mine. This is not something we can overlook, and we shall return to it. However, what interests us in the first instance is structured information, coded in a complex manner and meant to be interpreted.

We will distinguish three categories of elements that work in concert to make up information in the full sense of the concept. They are collectively present in all informational phenomena, and it is difficult to decide in which order they should be taken up. However, we will start in the order of their appearance in this introduction. We will call the ensemble MDE.

– A *message* is made up of coded signs that taken together make sense. The message may be transferred over different media. It may permit copying. It is intended to be read by a reading system.

– A reading or *decoding* system is a material entity that can decode the message. Such a system modifies its own state, and eventually produces an action outside itself, on matter. One of such actions could reproduce the message intended, or quite another message, different from the one intended.

– The *environment* is a setting in which the above action takes place and which itself produces some information from the fact of its action on the decoder.

The illustration of the cookery book recipe appears particularly apt. We all know that the three categories of the elements are going to work. They will produce the recipe as their message. The recipe has a history behind it. The decoder is the person who will create the dish: the cook or the chef. This person himself or herself has a history of their own. Finally, the environment is made up of diverse elements, including the location where the action is taking place, the available ingredients, the time available, the psychological atmosphere and so on. The environment might have been influenced by the person working in the kitchen, and by the fact that he or she was going to use the recipe. Certainly, we might find among other elements things that arose out of recipes that were used earlier. We also recognize the possibility that a single recipe could yield dishes that differ among themselves depending on the decoder (the cook) and the environment (the style of cooking and the ingredients).

In biology, the coded message is what is called *genetic information*. The cookery book recipe was a metaphor for the concept. However, one might risk overlooking an underlying reality if one were to treat all comparisons as metaphors. A classic instance of this possibility would be the theory of natural selection that Charles Darwin proposed in 1859. Darwin was inspired by the notion of selection, which today is described as artificial, but found to be valid by cattle farmers and nurserymen, and it was seen that a similar process existed in nature. That was a metaphor for most philosophers, but it was an extension of a concept for most biologists. For the latter, we can give a formal definition of the concept of selection that should both satisfy the evolutionist and accord with nature. The same process is at work in both cases. The fact that we have used the word "process" earlier for a human activity does not implicitly confer primacy on that aspect of the concept.

This does not appear to be an isolated instance of ambiguity. A natural process often cannot be fully understood if human industry has invented something to mimic it. It is said that William Harvey, circa 1628, had visualized the natural pacemaker for the heart in an age when pumps were being widely used. At the same time, a metaphor need not conceal an extension of a concept. In the following sections, a return to the cookery book recipe, and the other metaphors, need not hide the fact that the idea in the message applies equally well to the genome, and there will always be a decoder (human or not) and an environment to receive the message.

I.3. What is information?

Now it is not a question of giving a complete definition of information as it is of producing a plain outline of its characteristics that we consider of interest to us. Every sign can represent an element of information and generate an action. From a falling body that conveyed information as to the direction of its weight, to another whose state indicates temperature and to signals that can set off more or less automatic or reflex reactions, all will be considered to represent information.

What is relevant to life sciences is information coded in a message made up of a series of signs none of which means anything by itself, but an almost unlimited combination of which can design a multitude of things. Such information, as we have seen, is distributed between the message itself, the decoder and the environment. This information can replicate itself fairly faithfully and induce an action through the decoder. One such action, predictably and significantly, is the replication of the message itself. The languages out of those that have been found and studied are the human languages and those of the nucleic acids (DNA and RNA). We will see when we return to the concept of language that there are several other languages in nature. In particular, the functioning of ecosystems might conceal languages through which ecosystemic information might be constructed.

We have seen that a message is carried by a material entity. In the case of a message in a human language, the medium involved could be one of many types: the brain, a surface (stone, paper and so forth), a magnetic medium or data processing. The medium is much more homogeneous in the case of the genetic language. As far as we know, it is a nucleic acid: DNA or RNA. Technical progress in biology and data processing has in recent years enabled transfer of genetic information to a computer. Sequences of the DNA of bacteria have been read and stored in a computer's memory. This is what happened when they were modified and bundled into a new genome by engineers in Craig Venter's group. A genome was thus "written" into the computer, so that it synthesized a carrier chromosome of this genome. The chromosome was then introduced into a bacterium, and decoded in the usual manner and used. While a bacterium has not yet been synthesized, a genome has been. The point to note is that genetic information has been able to move through a computer, then to return in the DNA, and then serve as it would normally do.

At the base of the human language the elements are sounds, phonemes and signs written on media. Elementary sounds vary in number and content depending on the language. Linguists study all these aspects of language. As for the language of genetics, the four nucleotides of DNA and the four of RNA are still (to our knowledge) the same for all forms of terrestrial life (humans, in their usual humility, call them "universals"). These four signs, which collectively form the message of a nucleic acid, are the four nucleotides currently designated by the letters A, T, C and G for the DNA, and by A, U, C and G for the RNA. Molecular biology describes the functions of these elements.

The decoders of the human language are, of course, the human beings themselves. The collection of mechanisms with which the human being decodes a message and is able to transform it into action flows from a huge ensemble of disciplines: physiology, biochemistry, neurobiology, linguistics, psychology, biomechanics and so on. The mechanism by which the human being acquires the ability to achieve a particular task involves biological and social components, and, specifically, training in the language in which the message is coded. Another type of reading system developed with robotics. Robots are devices that make it possible to carry out tasks following human commands, which are in fact information programs. For the language of genetics, the reader is the living entity, and allows its genome expression. Elucidation of part of this decoder was a major scientific adventure of the 20th Century. The discovery of the *genetic code* (in the former sense, to which we shall return later) permits one to read the information carried by the DNA through a transcription in the RNA, and then a translation in protein. The discovery also allowed us to see how hereditary information was formed, transmitted and expressed. Let us, however, bear in mind that the information is collectively held in the ensemble *MDE*, which is made up of the *message* (the genome or the document), the reading system, which can *decode* the message (the living entity or its components) and the *environment*. Richard Charles "Dick" Lewontin called this the triple helix.

In this book, we start by examining information in the context that is the most natural for us: the human language. It would be interesting to begin by examining the prism of human and social relations, and then go on to the less familiar variations in animal communication. It seems reasonable that genetic information should open the discourse with different examples. We will try to stay clear of whatever new things biological languages might have brought to the concept of information. This position will encourage a fresh perspective on studies of ecological information. Ecosystems do carry information, but can we identify hidden ecological languages? Could languages of a new kind help us understand and manage our ecosystems better? We will end with a brief overview of information and the languages that code it. In this context, natural languages, refining and transmitting information, have sustained the various advances that have marked the different epochs of our planet, from its ecosystems right down to its denizens, and in particular, human beings and their cultures.

Acknowledgments

We would like to warmly thank Alan Bailur for his careful English translation and editing of a preliminary version of this text.

Human and Animal Communication

We, modern humans, find ourselves swimming in an ocean of information. If we were to get out of town to escape from the hubbub our fellow beings create, it may not be calm that awaits us in the forest. The forest has its own din, unceasing and of countless types. This is nature speaking to itself. Now, why should there be so much information being circulated, and so much time and energy being used up? This chapter discusses these questions, starting with the human case before going on to other languages in nature.

1.1. Language, that amazing thing

There are several ways in which *Homo sapiens* stand out from other species. Humans are bipeds, masters of fire, practitioners of art, makers of tools and weaponry, live well past the age of reproduction, impose rites of passage on each other between the stages of their life and so on. The human being is unique for many of these reasons. We differ from other primates in that we do not suffer from hirsuteness, and we walk on our rear limbs. However, there is another difference that, though rarely mentioned, is perhaps the most fundamental and the least anecdotal: *Homo sapiens* are information specialists. That is what this chapter is about, and we will also consider why this is the case.

Scientists of the 19th Century understood that *Homo sapiens* had not been created apart from other living beings, but was simply one among several species. Some, however, did not give up trying to find reasons for upholding our uniqueness, one way to try to regain our lost position. Many thoughtless assertions, such as "the human being is the only one to ...", have since been refuted. No, we are not the only ones to make tools; we are not the only ones to have a culture; we are not the only ones to know how to count. Chimpanzees and gray parrots can do some of these things. Saying that we do these things better, or that we can do more things than these, will not help save our ego as a species. The vanity evident in such beliefs is clearly unhealthy. It is a bit like the immaturity a child displays when they have not learnt that while they are unique, they are also equal to other children. In principle, difficult as it might be, the scientific approach should guard itself against the supposed uniqueness of the human species. At the same time, there is one striking fact we should not overlook.

Humans possess a characteristic that we may fail to notice, just as some of us may miss the elephant's trunk when we look at the animal or the activity of the dam-building beaver. *Humans talk*. They talk a great deal. In fact, talking or listening take up one-third of our waking time, that is more than 6 h a day. On average, we speak 16,000 words daily. The males of some bird species perhaps do better quantitatively, but our words, endlessly repeated, create meaning; they produce information.

In the context of language, information has a somewhat precise intuitive meaning: we know whether what we are hearing is interesting or boring. Even though such a subjective feeling does not by itself provide a usable measure for the quantity of information contained in a particular portion of speech, it does point out a significant lead. It is by modeling how we spontaneously measure the appeal of another individual's utterance that we can develop a general definition of the notion of information. This definition, though conceived in language, has applicability that extends well beyond.

1.2. The mechanics of language

Human communication is "monstrous" in several aspects, not only by the prohibitive amount of time devoted to it. Communication has requisitioned our memory and our intelligence. We know by heart tens of thousands of subtle shades of meaning found within words and expressions learnt during the course of our life. Any one of us can make an unlimited number of meaningful sentences using this lexicon, most of which may never have been uttered before. While we may be able to do this without much effort, we must not underestimate the intricacy of the mechanism involved. Language depends on incompletely understood processes, a study of which would be fascinating. The sentence "Last year, the alarm sounded when the birds flew overhead" provides illustrations of some of them. When we analyze the acoustic signal that reaches our ears, our brain recognizes some phonemes of English, the "l" of "Last", then the long vowel "ɑ:", then the "s" and so on. The sentences contain about 30 phonemes. Some of them, like "s", appear several times. These phonemes are drawn from a very limited set. English dialects offer a gamut of three dozens of them.

Why is it that there are so few phonemes? If there were more, every phoneme would have carried more information, our words would have been shorter and we would have been able to express numerically more ideas per minute. But this would have been at the cost of risking mounting confusion, because if we were to populate the accessible acoustic space of pronunciation with more phonemes, there would necessarily be a reduction in the acoustic contrasts that separate them. Then, why not enhance the acoustic contrast by utilizing fewer phonemes? After all, any computer scientist will tell you that two phonemes would do, as in Morse code. Yes, but then the words would grow longer, and they would flow more slowly. The English word "wonderful" is pronounced /'wʌndəfʊl/, and has eight phonemes, namely /w/, /ʌ/, /n/, /d/, /ə/, /f/, /ʊ/ and /l/. In the dot-and-dash Morse code, the word would read: dot dash dash space dash dash dash space dash dot space dash dot dot space dot space dot dash dot space dot dot dash dot space dot dot dash space dash dash dot dot, that is, 26 Morse signs and eight spaces. It is obvious that the two-phoneme code calls for a much longer stretch of time to transmit the word than the code composed of several phonemes within the acoustic space that our articulatory capacity allows us to access.

Phonology is a *code* that allows us to represent words in the form of sounds. Writing and sign languages are other codes that enable a representation of words. A code enables a transition from the domain of signs to the domain of meaning (Figure 1.1). The word "wonderful" may be coded by nine letters in writing, or by movements of the hand in the British sign language (both hands open, the index finger touching either side of the mouth, then moving forward and slightly outward). The meaning generated by these codes is the same.

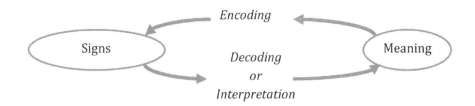

Figure 1.1. *A code enables a transition from the domain of signs to the domain of meaning*

Some codes are *word-for-word* codes. This is the case with the code used by underwater divers (Figure 1.2). Here, the code has about 10 different gestures, each with a very precise meaning. For example, "I have just exhausted my reserve of air". If there were no homophones in English, such as "hoard" and "horde", or synophones, such as "fare" and "fair", the phonological code would have been word-for-word.

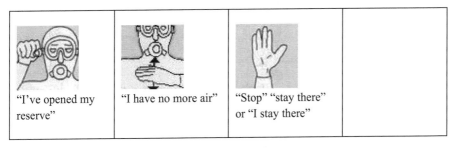

Figure 1.2. *The principal signs and their associated meanings in the code of underwater divers (http://www.aurel32.net/plongee/signes.php)*

The divers' code is not only word-for-word, but also *holistic*. In a holistic code, each sign is self-contained. It is not possible to break down the divers' code into elements that could then be reassembled into new gestures to form another code. Most codes of communication among primates appear holistic, and cries used for different meanings generally do not have common parts (Cheney and Seyfarth 1990). We shall have more to say on this aspect later. Holistic codes, however, show one limitation: an entirely new sign needs to be invented for each new meaning. It happens that nature invented a far more efficient system that is at work in our languages, and also in the biology of our cells: combinatorial codes.

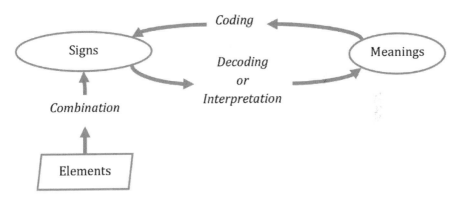

Figure 1.3. *Combinatorial coding*

In a *combinatorial* code, signs result from combinations of basic elements (Figure 1.3). The mechanism of combination is potentially capable of manufacturing a large number of signs. The phonological code is combinatorial: it manufactures its signs by combining phonemes. The word "wonderful" is encoded by a sign, /'wʌndəfʊl/, a combination of eight elementary phonemes. The system of traffic signs is combinatorial (Figure 1.4). The red circle stands for actions that are disallowed, the blue square for what is permitted and the red triangle warns of cyclists and other types of road user.

Figure 1.4. *Examples of partially combinatorial code:*
traffic signs © Crown copyright

Computer codes use combinations of bits (a bit taking either of the two values 0 or 1) as elements to form "words" that encode instructions to the processor or addresses in the memory. Binary words such as these used to have 8 bits in the earliest personal computers, but are generally encoded with 32 or 64 bits in present-day machines. The elements of the genetic code (Chapter 2) are the four molecules denoted as A, U, G and C, and these constitute RNA.

It is possible to superimpose several levels of codes. This is the case with human language. The sets of phonemes or, in writing, the sets of letters encode words, or more generally morphemes – carrier units of meaning. The word "speaking", for example, has two morphemes – a free morpheme *speak-*, the root, and a bound morpheme *-ing,* signifying a gerund form or a present participle. Sets of morphemes encode words according to the laws of morphology. In the above example, the two phonemes *speak-* and *-ing* together form the word *speaking*. Words, in turn, become elements of another code, the signs of which are phrases (nominal group, verbal group, etc.) and sentences. The hierarchy continues at higher linguistic levels: sentences go on to form discourses.

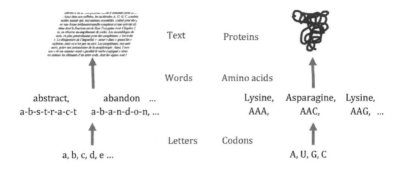

Figure 1.5. *Illustration of the parallel between the combinatorial hierarchies of written language and the living*

Figure 1.5 illustrates the principal levels of the combinatorial hierarchies that characterize written language and the living, placing the two alongside the combinatorics of molecular biology. The molecules A, U, G and C, constituents of RNA, are "read" in threes in our cells. This then results in the detection of codons that encode for amino acids, which in turn compose proteins. The proteins are molecules with the ability to assume a complex, three-dimensional form, and to perform a chemical activity. They carry out an essential part of the intelligent work within the cell (see Chapter 2).

The superimposition of combinatorial levels poses a problem, because such an action must be matched with a superimposition of the levels of code in order to set up a link between signs and meanings for each level. Figure 1.6 illustrates this notion for the decoding, and Figure 1.7 for the encoding. Consider the sentence "Last year, the alarms sounded when the birds flew overhead". The reader's brain analyzes the groups of typographic signs and isolates them: L-a-s-t y-e-a-r…, which it decodes into letters of the alphabet. It then composes the letters into words as "Last", "year" and so on. These words become the elements of a composite sign of a higher order, now made up of groups of words, and no more of letters. We have just carried out a complete turn of reading (Figure 1.6). Let us do a second round. The analysis of the groups of words isolates the words "when", "the", "birds" and so on, and our brain interprets them. It forms, for example, an image of birds; it associates the determiner "the" with the following noun, and sends out a simultaneous instruction for the word "when". It then composes meanings to form more complex representations, such as an image of birds in flight. These representations form a composite sign from a higher level. A third round of decoding will enable us to combine the images to portray causal relationships, for example. A fourth round will then allow us to have an understanding of the meaning of the complete story.

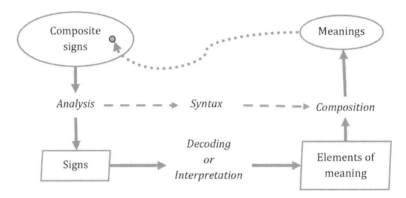

Figure 1.6. *Combinatorial decoding. The curved arrow shows how meanings at a level can serve as elements of a higher level*

Figure 1.6 illustrates the message–decoder–environment (MDE) principle discussed in the Introduction. The environment comes into play during the decoding of signs. When its role prevails, we would prefer the term *interpretation*. In its most basic form, the environment introduces errors or noise. However, it includes the decoder itself, its state and its history. In the case of a human listener or reader, their past knowledge and what they are looking for will exert a significant influence on how they understand a message. It must be remembered at the same time that it is impossible to determine what constitutes "relevant context", the constitution of which determines the result of the decoding. The sentence "There is water" will produce widely differing responses according to whether the respondent is an individual suffering from thirst in a desert or someone who has spotted a leak in his bathroom. We shall see, in Chapter 2, situations in which the presence of certain molecules in a cell, or the prior expression of certain portions of DNA, can significantly change the decoding of cells.

The decoding of the genome in our cells follows a hierarchy of mechanisms (Figure 1.5) that is organized as shown in Figure 1.6. We may describe the first analysis–decoding–composition cycle as follows: the RNA from the transcription of a portion of our DNA is analyzed by specialized molecules as a sequence of basic signs, that might be A, U, G or C, and is decoded as such. This decoding operation leads to a composition of these elements in sets of three and produces a meaning: the codon (there are 64 codons possible, see Chapter 2). The codons become the elements of a higher level decoding operation in which the codons are decoded in the form of amino acids, themselves compounded in the form of proteins. We can keep on traveling through the cycle, as shown in Figure 1.6: sets of proteins get analyzed, and then get interpreted by the cell in the form of their chemical affinities with other molecules. The meaning produced by the combination of these affinities is a graph or a network of chemical affinities. The higher levels of this decoding, which would see the networks of chemical affinity interact with one another, are still little understood. Modeling these levels of decoding will, however, be needed to establish a link between DNA and the overall structure of the cell.

A fundamental difference between human language and genetic code is that only the former is reversible. To put it another way, the cellular machinery is capable of extracting a meaning from the genetic sequence it reads in our DNA, but cannot write into it any meaning whatsoever. To create meaning, nature relies on random mutations and natural selection that places mutations in competition among themselves. Human language, at the same time, has the remarkable property of being able to encode meanings that can then be decoded. In order for this to work, the encoding and the decoding mechanisms must be similar (Figure 1.7).

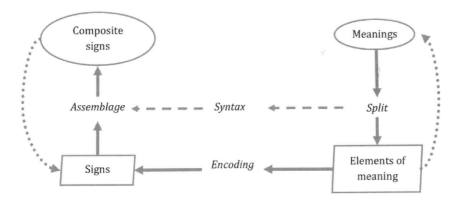

Figure 1.7. *Combinatorial encoding. The curved arrows indicate transitions in the hierarchic level*

In Figures 1.6 and 1.7, the link *syntax* represents the rules utilized in the structural assemblages. The simplest syntax consists of a simple juxtaposition. The phonemes or the codons are simply placed end to end during the operation of composition. However, the syntax can be much more sophisticated, as in the grammar of human languages.

1.3. What is syntax?

Combinatorial codes are generally characterized by constraints. In English, for instance, a *t* is not preceded by a *z* (*Aztec* is an exception, however it is not a native English word). In French writing, a *b* is not preceded by an *n* (except in the word *bonbon*). With some 30-odd phonemes that the language possesses (compared to the 44 that linguists assign to English), one can, in theory, produce unlikely sounds such as *k-d-k-d-i*. However, there are limits to how far such a process can go. Pronounceability is a factor that comes to mind. It is hard to conceive of a French speaker who can pronounce the word "kdkdi". Then there are rules governing pronunciation. As an example, the pairs of vowels *é-è, eu-e* and *au-o* follow a strict rule in the French spoken in southern France: they are open except when the vowel terminates the syllable. Consequently, words like *kerique* and *kelrique* can only occur in the French of southern France if they are pronounced "ké-rique" and "kèl-rique", the *é* and the *è* representing closed and open vowel sounds, respectively. Every language, every dialect and every accent possess their own phonological rules.

Phonological constraints reduce the throughput of information. The bar on closed vowels in the syllables *-kél-, -keul-* and *-kaul-* in the French spoken in the south diminishes the informational character of the vowels used. In the extreme case, if there were a single possibility for the vowels, it would be that they provide zero information, as their presence would be mandatory. If phonological constraints have the effect of diminishing information throughput, why should such constraints be there in the first place? Their existence is perhaps unrelated to any aspect of information, but has to do with ease of pronunciation or of learning.

When we speak or listen, we do not content ourselves with just recognizing the words uttered. We assign particular meanings to groups of words. "Last year" and "Next year" bring to mind different meanings. Words are therefore elements of a code of an upper hierarchic level in which signs are sentences (Hauser 1996), or sometimes those which are not quite sentences. A string such as "Birds fly look" may have a meaning in certain contexts, but an English speaker could fault it on grounds of syntactic correctness. This is because language places certain constraints on combinations of words.

What is the purpose of *syntax*? A short answer would be that syntax is a set of rules governing the way words are used, and this implies certain constraints on how they are uttered or written. An observable effect of syntactic constraints is to limit the range of possible word combinations. While one may say "When flew the birds" (obviously sounding literary), one may not say "Flew when the birds". Syntactic constraints are strict. The 10 words of the sentence "Last year, when the birds flew overhead, the alarm sounded" can be combined in 3,628,800 different ways, but only a handful of them are considered syntactically acceptable.

Syntax does not owe its existence to its role as censor for the forms it considers incorrect, even though some of them might make sense. It has a higher task, which is to enable an encoding-decoding operation with sets of words (Figures 1.6 and 1.7). The sentences "Peter hit Paul" and "Paul hit Peter" both have the same words, but do not mean the same thing. Syntax guides us to an understanding of (in this example) who did what and to whom. More generally, syntactic structure introduces asymmetric dependencies between words or groups of words. The difference in meaning between "the cousin of his neighbor" and "the neighbor of his cousin" arises from the order of the groups of words. If such order were absent, the interpretation of the combination "cousin/neighbor" would have been arbitrary. The prepositional phrase "of his cousin" depends on the noun phrase "his neighbor". Our capacity for interpretation uses such asymmetric dependencies in order to build meanings.

1.4. Meaning

Language code is not word-for-word. The semantic decoding of a sentence, that is, the determination of its meaning, presupposes the execution of a process of interpretation that researchers in the science of language have not modeled completely (Dunbar 1996). Consider the sentence: "Last year, the alarms sounded when the birds flew overhead". One interpretation of the temporal relations of this sentence would be that there were several flights of birds and that the alarm sounded several times, probably at the moment of each flight. We might even imagine a causal relation between each flight of birds and the sound of the alarm. Collecting the meanings of the words "birds", "flew", "alarm" and "sounded" will not be enough if we are to properly interpret the sentence. It is not as if we were playing with a building-block set. We have to carry out a calculation, taking into account the typical duration of birds' flights and of the ringing of the alarm, and comparing them to a particular year, before we can decide whether this particular episode was a repetition of an earlier one. Consider "Last year, when I was repairing my roof, my car's petrol tank sprang a leak". Here, in this example, the two episodes referred to may be unique ones and may not have any causal relationship. The construction of the meaning of a statement (Figure 1.6) impacted its interpretation, not so much its decoding. The reason for this is that knowledge outside the statement, in the form of the environment and the listener or reader, entered the scene.

The calculation of a meaning is an instinctive process, most often performed without much effort. What is the result of that process? These questions have engaged the attention of philosophers for a long time. Cognitive sciences have cast some light on them, and this has had the merit that testable theories have emerged, alongside devices that successfully reproduce the human capacity for interpretation, though admittedly modest in scale at the present time. From a cognitive point of view, there is no difference between the natures of meaning and perception. The interpretation of "The book that is on my desk, on top of the pile" is a perception, relatively limited for someone who has not seen the said desk, but possibly clear enough to enable him/her to find the book in question. The person tasked with bringing the book back will have to adjust two perceptions: the direct view of the desk in a state of disorder and the perception created by the statement. The interpretation of "… when the birds flew …" also made use of our capacity for temporal and spatial perceptions.

The interpretation of a statement does not end with its meaning. To be able to understand the statement on the birds, the listener will need to form an image of birds flying by the volumetric detector of the alarm in the narrator's house. However, the listener will go beyond that point, and probably infer a causal relationship between the flight of the birds and the triggering of the alarm.

1.5. Beyond meaning

Production of meaning is not the first function of statements. If it were, we would have been passing our time uttering long strings of stupid, but completely meaningful, statements of the type "The carpet is gray/there are four lamps in this room/it was night when the sun set". Meaning is only a means in the service of a much higher object, which is to raise interlocutors' interest. This notion of interest is critical in defining the concept of information (Dessalles 2013).

Our natural speech is composed of sounds that enable us to recognize morphemes. Morphemes in turn combine to make recognition of words possible, and words are arranged so as to form sentences, which in turn go on to create meaning. How does *meaning* come about? In spontaneous human conversation, meaning is generated by two principal activities: the evocation of an event and the production of an argument. These two conversational behaviors, narration and argumentation, cover more than 90% of our time in spontaneous speech. Narration consists of reporting events, that is, the where and when of happenings, putting in perspective the facts of given situations and of the protagonists concerned (Galtung and Ruge 1965). Argumentation is quite different. It does not resurrect a situation, but deals with problems, that is contradictions contained in statements made, involving observations, beliefs or wishes.

Language is thus a "game" that possesses two aspects, sometimes overlapping but largely independent, on the cognitive plane: evocation and logic. The two corresponding behaviors, namely narration and argumentation, are found in extreme and ritual forms in news and debates that different media have (Galtung and Ruge 1965). News items are stories relative to events, recent most often, while debates deal with problems that result from conflicting beliefs or intentions. The word *information* is naturally associated with the two aspects of language: on the one hand, the events may contain information, while, on the other, the element that enables a resolution of a problem may also be called information.

Information, in the sense of the word that we are going to adopt, covers both of these aspects. Information brings about a change in the observer's access to the situation that he/she is considering. It is through language that we try to modify the cognitive state of our interlocutors. They measure the interest, and therefore the information, that our discourse holds based on the magnitude of this change (Galtung and Ruge 1965; Dessalles 2013). However, this should not create the impression that the notion of information only applies to human discourse.

1.6. Non-human languages

In mathematics, the word *language* designates the type of combinatorial code described in Figure 1.1. A formal language utilizes elements that may be combined into signs (we are speaking here of *words*) such that they may be made subject to rules of grammar. Clearly, this definition applies to *natural* human languages. It would apply even better to artificial human languages, such as Java, C++, Prolog or Python. Would it do equally well describing communication among the living?

Living beings, animal or vegetal, complex or unicellular, produce and acquire information. The cells in our bodies send signals, in the shape of hormones, to other cells; butterflies emit pheromones to attract sexual partners; ants have a huge armory of substances that they leave on the soil for their sisters. Communication among the living can use all the dimensions for which the sender has available to the recipient: chemical, visual, olfactory, vibratory and so on. What about language? As far as we know, communication among ants is not combinatorial. As in the case of divers, their chemical signs do not lead to systematic combinations. Pheromones are easily analyzable, like molecules or atoms, but they are essentially chance assemblages. The purists will refuse to talk about the language of ants, except metaphorically.

Combinations are widely found in animal communication. The male nightingale, for example, has a repertory of some 200 songs that can be analyzed into superimposed combinatorial levels: the bird emits a sequence of calls, "the context", made up of "packages"; each packet is a memorized combination of "songs", which are composed of simpler elements, "sections" (Hauser 1996, p. 286). The multiple combinations evolved to the present level of complexity because the females of the bird species are able to decode the presence of each package, each song and each section when setting the males competing. Likewise, male birds being able to borrow stanzas of their neighbors' songs show that they have already decoded them. We may therefore quite legitimately talk about language here.

We can hear the critics already. The language of nightingales is not semantic: it does not carry specific meanings beyond: "I am the superb male" or "This territory is mine". We may retort that every sign has a meaning when it is decoded. It is true, of course, that contrary to what humans impose on their language, the nightingales' calls are not expected to evoke perceptions. Their calls may apparently say nothing about the tree or the pond or a neighboring nightingale. This type of referential communication, able to evoke perceptions, is indeed present in nature, if not among nightingales. Historically, it was a study of bees that showed this to be clearly true.

Since ancient times, beekeepers have known that bees communicate among themselves about the location of food sources. However, so long as the code they used remained unknown, the ability to do this appeared magical. What, by the way, is the "language" of the bees? An answer became available in the 1940s when Karl von Frisch cracked the code of the language of the bees (Von Frisch 1953), a discovery that brought him the Nobel Prize. A bee visits the cupful of sugared water that the investigator has placed at some distance from the hive. She returns to the hive and performs a characteristic dance for her sisters on the honeycomb in the darkness of the hive. The dance follows a straight line along which the bee rapidly swings her abdomen back and forth. Then she returns to where she started from, turning right and left alternately, and then resumes her swinging in a straight line. The entire series of movements produces a characteristic trajectory (Figure 1.8). Now, what is remarkable is that the angle formed by the path of the dance movement with the vertical line mimics the angle formed by the sun's direction with the direction of the path to the source of food. Even more remarkable is the fact that the dancing bee, seeking to enlist her sisters in the foraging for food, might carry on dancing for several minutes or even hours. The position of the sun will have changed while this goes on, but the bee keeps pace with every change by varying the angle of her dance. In the 1990s, researchers were able to send bees into predetermined locations by placing miniaturized robots that simulated the oscillating dance (Kirchner and Towne 1994). Thus, we had evidence of having understood the code of bees.

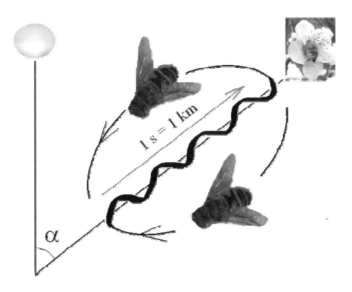

Figure 1.8. *Illustration of the trajectory of a bee in her hive, which she uses to show to her sisters a source of food (http://commons.wikimedia. org/wiki/File: Bee_dance.png). For a color version of this figure, see www.iste.co.uk/gaucherel/information.zip*

Does the way bees communicate among themselves constitute a language? The signs that show the directions to take in foraging for food form a continuum, with the values of the angle between the axis of the dance and the vertical varying continuously. This is a rich way of communication, even if it has not been formed by a combination of simpler elements. A language theorist may only see in it a holistic code, but the code of the bees is in fact much more than that. It is an *analog* code, that is a continuously varying code. Some sign language also show gradual properties. The sign for falling can also include signs relating to the speed or trajectory of the fall. Spoken language offers instances of an analog code: "These children are *imppppossible*!". The analog code of the bees shares a characteristic with human languages, namely arbitrariness. In this language, the vertical replaces the direction of the sun and the direction of the path of the dance takes the place of the direction of the flight. These arbitrary choices recall the arbitrary character of our own words.

Another reason that leads us to view the code of the figure of 8 dance of the bees as a language is that it is compositional. Compositionality is a property of some combinatorial codes. In a compositional code, the meaning of a combination of signs may be deduced from the meaning of the signs that exist in its components (Figure 1.6). Human languages are compositional: the meaning of a sentence can be deduced from the words that constitute it even when the context intervenes. There are exceptions. Certain idiomatic expressions, such as "kick the bucket", "pass the buck", "get the sack" and "keep one's shirt on", have meanings quite different from the sum of the meanings of the individual words used. This is especially the case when their etymology has been lost. Idioms are therefore not compositional. The code of the bees has compositionality of a particular type: the length of the straight path of the dance provides the measure of the distance to be traveled. This indication is to be combined with the indication of the angle to obtain the location of the source of food.

Closer to home in the genealogy of species, there are examples of codes both referential and compositional at the same time. Many varieties of macaques emit alarm calls when they see a predator. Vervet monkeys emit calls that differ with whether they have spotted an eagle, a snake, a leopard or another troop of Vervets (Cheney and Seyfarth 1990). Another species, Campbell's Mona Monkey, combines the same vocal signals for such different events as the fall of a branch, the presence of a leopard or the presence of another troop of its own kind (Zuberbühler 2006).

1.7. Types of language

We have just identified some properties that languages may possess. Some languages, even the most developed, such as the nightingale's song, only produce a single meaning, generally continuous, that corresponds to a certain quality that the signal permits to be registered. Other languages, such as the alarm system of Vervet monkeys, produce several meanings. Then there are languages that rely on a production of combinations. Table 1.1 contains some examples of languages classified according the following criteria: *unique* or *multiple* meanings, combinatorial signal system, presence of a *syntax*. A signal, such as the call of the deer, produces a continuous index that is evaluated by the females of the species (Figure 1.9(a)). Signals with the same meaning can be combined. This happens with secondary sexual traits of the domestic rooster: his colorful comb, plumage and song combine without producing any meaning other than an assertion of the quality of maleness (Figure 1.9(c)). The song of the nightingale also produces (as far as we know) a single meaning, a performance level other nightingales can measure. The song is combinatorial, combining as it does a collection of simpler elements, and obeys a syntax that makes it characteristic (Figure 1.9(e)). It is essentially digital, being constructed of elements that the bird has the option to insert or omit. The complex nuptial routine that birds (such as ducks) must go through before mating obeys a similarly strict syntax, even if its meaning remains simple and unique.

In systems of multiple meanings, combinatorial signals match the range of meanings. The alarm calls of Vervet monkeys apparently lack any combinatorial character (Figure 1.9(b)) (Zuberbühler 2006). The dance of bees produces several meanings pertaining to locations by combining the angle of the path of the dance with length and the number of oscillations (Kirchner and Towne 1994). A similar combination of meanings is seen in the pidgins which are languages without syntax produced when adults need to communicate with the help of a vocabulary of a language that is not their own (Bickerton 1990). Thus, "Demain moi retour campagne" ("Tomorrow me return country"), said in Tai-boi (a pidgin of Indochina), carries the same meaning regardless of the order of the words. A language is called *compositional* if meanings depend, and depend uniquely, on a combination of signs (Figure 1.9(c)). The dance of the bees and the pidgins appear to be compositional codes. This statement is valid, however, only if the constraint "depend uniquely" is applied without insisting on rigor. When the interpretation involves the context (the environment in the MDE schema), the code ceases to be compositional in a strict sense. We may consider that a language is compositional when different meanings can be deduced from different combinations of signs. With this more flexible definition, pidgins can be seen to be indisputably compositional. A language that has expressions with multiple meanings, but is not compositional, is called *holistic*: it must have a distinctive sign (or a sign with only incidental resemblances to other signs) for every meaning (Figure 1.9(b)).

In a compositional language, syntax not only governs the structure of combinations, but also establishes the link between this structure and the meaning produced (Figure 1.9(f)). In human languages, meanings possess a structure. If we imagine that Peter hit Paul, we believe that Peter is the actor, and Paul the patient of the action of being hit. These relations occur in a syntactic structure: the actor is here designated the subject, the patient the complement, while the action (the predicate) is indicated by the verb. Note that the syntax–semantics correspondence is not always quite as immediate, if we recall the example of the flight of the birds. In a compositional syntactic language, such as a human language (but not a pidgin), the structure of the message provides information on the structure of the meaning.

Unique meaning	*Non-combinatorial*		Deer's bell
	Combinatorial	*No syntax*	Collection of secondary sexual traits
		Syntax	Song of a nightingale courtship displays
Multiple meanings	*Holistic*		Cry of alarm
	Combinatorial (compositional)	*No syntax*	Dance of bees Pidgin
		Syntax	Human language

Table 1.1. *Classification of types of language*

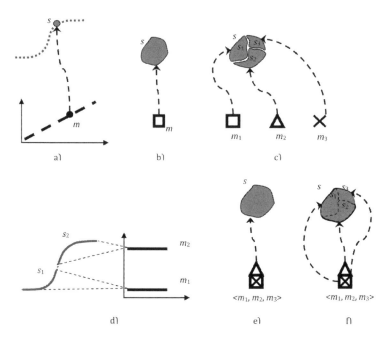

Figure 1.9. *Pictorial representation of types of signifier–signified relations. a) Analog type: the variation of the signifier (m) is in correspondence with the variation of the signified (s), b) holistic type: a signifier for each signified, c) compositionality: the signified is inferred from the juxtaposition of the signifiers, d) quantization: discrete signifiers for a continuous signified, e) non-compositional syntax and f) compositional syntax. For a color version of this figure, see www.iste.co.uk/gaucherel/information.zip*

Of the greatest interest to linguists and computer scientists is the type of syntax that governs the structure of sign combinations. The syntax of the call of a bird can be represented using a simple procedure (called *finite state machine*) that requires little memory, while the syntax of human languages makes significant demands on memory (we are speaking here of central recursion, Hauser *et al.* 2002). For example, in the sentence "My cousin's neighbor who lives in Paris is an engineer", the subordinate clause "who lives in Paris" is embedded in the noun phrase "My cousin's neighbor who lives in Paris", which is itself part of the global clause "My cousin's neighbor … is an engineer". As far as we know, human language is the only one that uses nestings or embeddings as this example shows.

Table 1.1 does not contain all the distinctions that exist among languages. An interesting difference is that between the analog language (Figure 1.9(a)) and the digital language (Figure 1.9(d)). Table 1.2 shows these differences in the case of combinatorial languages. Digital combinatorial languages depend on combinations of fixed elements. This is so in the case of words that are sets of phonemes, and sentences which are sets of words (or of morphemes). Conversely, the language of bees gives an indication of the direction in an analog manner, since the angle concerned varies with the direction.

Analog	Angle of the path of the bee's dance
Digital	Nightingale's song Words of a human language Sentences from a human language

Table 1.2. *Analog and digital compared*

One of the essential qualities of a digital code is that it resists being copied multiple times. It is therefore not surprising to find digital characteristics in human languages, in which messages are tossed about by word of mouth, and similarly in the transmission of molecular heredity (see Chapter 2), in which messages are transmitted from one generation to another. Another purpose digital codes serve is to prepare for a combination in which each element is either present or absent.

Figures 1.6 and 1.7 show, respectively, the structure of the decoding hierarchy and reversibility, elements that were excluded from Table 1.1. Another difference between languages, just as fundamental as the others, relates to the arbitrary character of the signs. This property presupposes a radical independence between the sign and its meaning. Some codes are not arbitrary. This is particularly so with indicators of quality that are competitive signals (the bellow of a deer or the plumage of a peacock) for which there must be a link between performance and meaning (or quality). Analog signals are never wholly arbitrary, because there remains an iconic relationship with the signified. For example, in the case of the dance of the bees, the choice of the vertical direction to represent the path of the sun is arbitrary, provided that the variations of the angle are necessarily linked to the indications of the direction of the flight.

Some of the properties we have just mentioned logically come before some of the others (Figure 1.10). An arbitrary code, for example, will result from an iconic code by drift. A digital code may evolve by quantization (thresholding) and simplification from a simple analog code. Quantization may operate in any gradual field (sound amplitude, frequency, duration, etc.). The elements of a holistic code may, in principle, be split, that is cut in time; if the resulting fragments can be rearranged in different combinations, we obtain a combinatorial code: this is how the complex song of a bird can become progressively more complex from simpler song elements. This mechanism, though, has little chance of being able to produce a compositional code, because it would involve the splitting of the signifier and the signified at the same time. A compositional code has a better chance of evolving through a superimposition of referential designations, each relating to a part of the designated position (Dessalles 2010). The two systems, the combinatorial and the compositional, may both use digital elements (Figure 1.10). Lastly, a syntax may develop simply because the combinatorial system producing the signal is constrained: this may be the case with a non-referential code, such as birdsong. For a referential code, and for the relationships among signals, a syntax will emerge to express a preexisting structure in the designated situation.

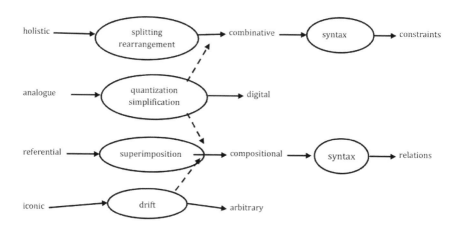

Figure 1.10. *Derivational relationships between codes*

1.8. Why give information?

Information is a useful thing to have when it is reliable and useful for whoever decodes it. But why should it be good to give it? The answer is simple in the case of two sexual partners: the interests of the sender and the receiver coincide at least partially. Members of a family similarly share common interests. We can understand what drives bees to communicate with one another: the fact that they are sisters. While remaining within the framework of natural selection, we need to only think at the level of genes, and not at the level of individuals, to convince ourselves of the benefit for which the bee performs her dance. A genetic mutation that enables a more precise performance will not be of much use to the bee as an individual, as she would lose more time doing a higher level of dancing. However, the mutation may spread because the beneficiaries of the information are sisters of the dancer, and most of them will have had a similar mutation. In other words, the mutation is beneficial to copies of itself. Likewise, the alarm call of the black-and-white colobus benefits his family (Zuberbühler 2006). As in the case of bees, the genes that determine patterns of behavior in the face of danger are transmitted to the offspring of colobus, even though the one issuing the alarm lowers his/her chances of survival by attracting the predator's attention.

The community of interest between sender and receiver is more frequent than generally thought. It might even exist in unexpected contexts, say between predator and prey. It explains the behavior, strange at first sight, of a Thompson's gazelle within sight of a lion. The gazelle will naturally take flight, but will first perform some spectacular leaps in the air (stotting). Most of us have seen photos of these gazelles in Africa jumping to great heights, and expending their energy in the act. That amount of energy would certainly have been more useful in the animals' flight, and therefore for their survival. Ethologist Amotz Zahavi has analyzed the scenario in an original manner (Zahavi and Zahavi 1997). According to him, the gazelle, in leaping up into the air, is sending the lion a signal that can only be characterized as honest. The lion has every reason to believe the information that its potential prey has provided. According to Zahavi, that information is that the gazelle is fully fit, and that the lion would in all probability be wasting its time engaging in a chase. This information is honest, because the gazelle could not be lying, if only because she has vaulted to the height that she could reach. An individual not at the peak of fitness could not accomplish such a feat, and a mediocre performance would send a very clear message to the lion: "Chase me!" We can see here how natural selection produces an honest communication between prey and predator, granting that their interests diverge on all other planes.

A strange phenomenon, pointed out by biologists John Krebs and Richard Dawkins, can also arise in the evolution of a communication, where the sender and the receiver do not have the same or similar interests (Krebs and Dawkins 1984). The receipt of information by the receiver is a good starting point for a study of this phenomenon. Let us say there is a male dog that senses that another dog is about to pounce on him and bite him. He has thus gathered information about the intentions of the second dog. The second dog, quite unexpectedly, has a certain power over the first, in that he can manipulate him, lead him to believe that he will launch an attack, while in fact he does not intend to. It would be in the first dog's interest, then to wait for reliable indications of the second dog's intentions, such as flexing his legs to prepare for an attack or baring his teeth. The second dog would find it in his interest to mimic the first dog's behavior, even though he may not have intended an attack in the first place. Such a reading/manipulation association evolves into sufficiently exaggerated signals to put off the least credulous observer. We have passed from a discreet flight of information to a clamorous climax in manipulation. For Krebs and Dawkins, the exaggerated signals met with in nature would lead to such a dialectic of reading/manipulation. It comes back to a dual operation, namely use of the sender by the receiver and vice versa. The song of the nightingale, the peacock's plumage and even some human rituals, at least in part, could have resulted from this mechanism.

In many situations, the interests of the sender appear to be non-existent, so that communication remains a mystery. The Vervet's call of alarm is intended for the entire troop. Why is it that the Vervets are not content to benefit from the alarms sent by other species that would have guarded them from the attention of the predator? Zahavi, who has studied the desert-dwelling Arabian babbler species for decades, explains the strange behavior of the members of a species while communicating among themselves as an act of publicity (Zahavi and Zahavi 1997). The Arabian babbler species has the habit of mobbing predators. If a snake appears, the little birds form a ring around it, and threaten to attack it with their beaks. Such behavior can hardly be safe, since the snake's mouth is not far. In sound Darwinian logic, one would have expected each bird to leave the job of mobbing the predator to its companions, a behavior that ought to have disappeared after several generations. However, this has not been the case. According to Zahavi, the harassment inflicted on the snake is not intended for the reptile, but is in fact meant for members of the flock! In the act of daring the predator, each member of the flock is showing off its courage. The information such displays convey is crucial in the world of this species: every member of the flock now knows who are the brave ones when it comes to choosing one's friends and allies.

Figure 1.11. *An Arabian babbler (Turdoides squamiceps). For a color version of this figure, see www.iste.co.uk/gaucherel/information.zip*

This is not an instance of anthropomorphism. The lifespan of an Arabian babbler is at least 60 years, which it spends in the shelter of one of the scarce shrubs that thrive in the desert, thereby escaping from raptors. Outside that shelter, the bird's lifespan drops to under 2 years. The worst enemy of the Arabian babbler is not the raptor: the main danger to the bird comes from other Arabian babblers that may dislodge it from the bush it occupies. The first thing the bird must do is team up with brave fellow birds capable of taking risks in defending their bush home from invaders. If one were to follow Zahavi, the behavior the birds show toward the snake is very much a signal, and the information it conveyed is social in nature. This could prove to be a costly signal, as there is high risk in harassing a predator. The worst losers are those who abstain from action, because by not offering information about their courage they may fail to be recruited, and consequently risk being excluded from all bushes in the area.

The story of the Arabian babbler should serve to alert us about the operation of the numerous types of animal behavior, and even human behavior. The alarm call of the Vervet monkey may well have a social function, such as making known the individual's suitability for sentry duty, something that might incline its fellow Vervets toward keeping it in the troop. What can we say about human inclinations toward providing information?

Individuals of our species are extremely fond of information. They pay to receive it, and at the same time they are in a hurry to dispense it. The nearly 16,000 words we utter on average each day are evidence of this. Why do we behave in this way?

The web is a product of our appetite for information. Its beginnings date back to the 1990s. The scientists who brought into being the first web pages were simply looking to facilitate access to technical documentation within their group. The story would have ended there. The Minitel in France carried out this function of providing access to information. There was one essential difference, however: users of the Minitel could not *provide* information, but only receive it. Though unintended, the stroke of genius of the inventors of the web lay in offering to each individual, and in particular to the scientists who had computer access, an opportunity to create a page of their own. And what an explosion that caused! Instead of putting out simple technical manuals, scientists could now make use of the system to display their articles. Then it was the turn of the public. Everyone could provide information and benefit by displaying themselves. The rest is history: an explosion in the number of web pages, appearance of blogs and the arrival of social networking platforms.

The Twitter network is a perfect example of how information is exchanged in our species. A Twitter subscriber can post short messages that are received by "followers", i.e. other subscribers wishing to receive what the first has to say. And that system has been working. Subscribers devote a prodigious amount of time in posting messages about events they have personally witnessed, and to forward messages they receive and find interesting. This type of network is the best propagator of news and current rumors. Twitter subscribers are not paid for their labors. This is not strictly an exchange, since the majority (80%) of the follower–followed links are asymmetric (Kwak *et al.* 2010). Twitter subscribers, like all other human beings, provide information because they like to do it. Twitter broadens the narrative function of language by enabling users to minimize the passage of time between an event and narration. How should one explain this narrative reflex, unique in nature because of its scale and systematic character?

After having long ignored the issue of treating language activity as a necessary corollary of intelligence, scientists recently recognized the importance of the problem. They had earlier believed that information was the subject of cooperation, or of a swapping arrangement, or a matter of give-and-take. "If you scratch my back, I'll scratch yours". This description is obviously not valid when applied to the provision of information, as opposed to the performance of a service. We generally do not behave like spies, or punters, or speculators on the stock market, who exchange information worth money on the basis of a perfect reciprocity. People not only dispense information willingly, but compete with one another to do so. The important thing is to be the first. What is more, such information most often relates to trivial matters. Take a look at Twitter. Human communication has little to do with a give-and-take type of exchange, but much more to do with showing that we are the first to know and tell.

Where did this behavior come from? The analogy of Zahavi's Arabian babblers may contain an answer. We provide information to our fellow beings, not for its own value, but as a means of flaunting our ability to acquire it, much like how the birds show off their courage in teasing their potential predator. It still remains to be explained how this ability has a social value in human society.

Primatologist Robin Dunbar observed that language is deeply involved in the establishment and preservation of social relations (Dunbar 1996). His studies led him to hypothesize that language would have replaced grooming, a practice that plays the role of cementing relationships among numerous species of primate, including those closest to us. Instead of spending time picking through the fur of other members of the troop, which is what the primates do, human beings spend their hours together talking. Could it be that language is the human equivalent of grooming among primates? It certainly makes for an appealing hypothesis, but there should be added room in it to accommodate an explanation of why human conversation largely consists of narration of events, rather than a series of synchronized grunts.

Here, the parallel of the Arabian babbler may turn out to be useful, if we bear in mind certain traits of our species. The Arabian babbler adopts an entire series of costly behaviors, starting with the harassment of its predator, so as to form alliances and so protect others in the flock. The bird's situation is not unlike ours. As the Latin dramatist Plautus observed over 2,000 years ago, man is wolf to man, and this suggests an even more dramatic scenario.

For the first time in history, our distant ancestors had found a means of killing their fellow beings without particular risk to themselves. Having discovered weapons such as stones and pointed sticks, the hominids were able to kill their congeners by surprise. The discovery inevitably upset the inherited social order of the primates that was founded on superiority of muscles. In the case of chimpanzees, the alpha male, that is the male at the top of the hierarchy, fathers between 30% and 40% of the next generation (Reynolds 2005). Imagine in this context that killing without risk is possible. The male ranked third in the order can easily rise in rank, using surprise to kill the alpha male and the beta male, and then becoming the one to procreate the most progeny. That would be a possibility, unless of course he got killed instead!

The only safeguard against the eventuality of murder by surprise would be to surround oneself with friends able to ensure protection against danger. This is perhaps why in our species information has replaced muscle. By displaying to those around us the most surprising events, we are showing all through the day our superior ability to acquire information, marking us out as good potential allies or friends. As in the case of the Arabian babblers, we parade a quality that will make us look good in the eyes of our congeners. This quality, this informational capability, has become crucial because of the particular "political ecology" of our species. This explanation of the importance of information in our case is one of the few that has the merit of being consistent, on the one hand with the reality of language and, on the other hand, compatible with the constraints of Darwinian theory.

1.9. The autonomy of information

The propensity of human beings to peddle information creates a space in which certain information appears, circulates and then vanishes. According to an analogy suggested by Richard Dawkins, information travels between brains a little like genes within generations or viruses among individuals. In this analogy, the substrate consisting of the accumulation of humankind's brains serves as the biotope for a particular fauna that Dawkins calls "memes" (Dawkins 1976). Memes are elements of information of different types: events, beliefs and opinions, all capable of passing from one brain to another, as if by contagion. This movement of information is the theatre of a form of selection, a mirror image of what happens to living beings. The more infectious the memes, the better they propagate. Opposing memes fight for supremacy. Some memes will sink into oblivion, and die, while others may mutate as a result of wrong transmission, and so on.

The theory of memes, like all analogies, does have its limitations, but it is an interesting source of inspiration. Its defenders will say that the theory is itself a meme, having shown itself as particularly infectious since its invention by Dawkins in 1976. One of its limitations is that it ignores meme hosts and their cognitive constraints. The informational value of memes depends on cognitive computations that our brain most often carries out unconsciously. Knowledge of these cognitive processes will undoubtedly make better predictions about the spread of memes than is possible with the simple analogy of contagion. We will examine some of these processes to better understand the specificity of the information of human origin.

In the 1960s, some journalistic studies attempted to identify the factors that make information interesting. The result was a catalog of factors such as the unexpected, reference to personages from the elite, cultural proximity, and intense character. A cognitive approach would reduce the catalog to two principal factors: emotional value *a priori* and unexpectedness.

The emotional value *a priori* gives the scale of interest to which reference is made. The semantics of the event tell us whether we are talking of life or of death, of lay-offs, or a win of 10 euros. We are interested in events in each of these scales without comparing them. However, emotion *a priori* is insufficient to generate interest. Every moment, there is a death, or someone loses her job, or someone wins 10 euros. We do not consider these events as subjects of information. There is one essential ingredient missing here: the interest we have in information as necessarily due to our perception of *unexpectedness*.

Intuition tells us that unexpectedness implies low probability. An accident happening to a loved one, a birthday coincidence, an explosion in the neighborhood, a fire on the Eiffel Tower and a celebrity in a restaurant, all of these situations interest us, and we speak about them. They constitute for us and our near ones information. Subjectively, we perceive these situations as improbable, and therefore unexpected. The probability concept is not adequate in dealing with the unexpected, because probability theory does not take account of the egocentric character of unexpectedness. As we shall see in Chapter 4, unexpectedness is measured by the abnormal simplicity of the event to the observer. We all know the saying, "accidents only happen to others". The others, who are anonymous by definition, are hard to describe. If it is a colleague who is a victim, even a colleague you may not have known personally, concern and emotion grow with their proximity to you, whether they work in the same company, in the same building, in the same service, or have the same birthday as you. Likewise, the Eiffel Tower or celebrities are well known enough for the events concerning them to have emotional impact, and therefore to possess information.

The same phenomenon explains why information is a perishable good. Few individuals take the trouble to read newspapers older than 3 days. An old event, say the assassination of President Kennedy, is not information anymore, because its cognitive reach has become complex. This event has receded into the lists we maintain in our memory: the chronological list of events, the list of historic events arranged in order of importance, the list of the presidents of the United States and the list of assassinations. At the time of the 15th anniversary of the death of President Kennedy, the event has become a piece of information, only because access to it has become easier – a half-century is simpler than say 47 years 3 months and 2 days. The anniversary thus creates a shortcut in the access to the memory of the event, and our interest in it is automatically awakened.

Life and the spread of information depend on purely cognitive factors. Dates of anniversaries have nothing to do with the contagious nature of the meme. Among the cognitive factors that influence information, and often threaten its existence, there is, of course, critical thought. Information has credibility that may vary across time and with individuals. Information that is no longer credible loses its informational character. We doubt certain information because we possess the ability to spot logical inconsistencies. We would, for instance, find it difficult to believe that Cuba was able to provide to the United States important information on Venezuela, because such news would contradict our knowledge of the current diplomatic relations between these countries.

This ability to detect inconsistencies between facts and beliefs is a typically human faculty, and probably quite unique among the living. It may have evolved in our species as a protective mechanism against deceit. We owe to it, among other things, our ability to reason. Without it, all the information available at any given time would be worthless. Without logical tests of consistency, the only information we would turn our attention to would be that directly verifiable through our senses. The world would then become one of here-and-now. Such a world, that might have been the world of our ancestors, stood shattered with the emergence of our critical capacity. Unverifiable information attracted interest since it could be examined for credibility. At some point in its evolution, our species entered a world of elsewhere (in time and space). As we shall see in the following chapters, the ability to withdraw ourselves from the local world and the current moment is also a feature of biological and ecological information.

Because of our logical abilities, we only verify, visually, a tiny part of the information that we accept. The information circulating on the cerebral biotope of the human species is placed on a narrow (though infinite) fringe, that is constituted of facts that are both unexpected and consistent with the known. In every case, information is conveyed by language, and only exists in the eye of the beholder. Is it possible to generalize this concept of information so as to cover cases in which the human being and its language are not involved?

1.10. Language and information

For a mathematician, a language is grounded in a combinatorial code. The code of the bees is hardly combinatorial, and yet we happily speak of the language of the bees! The signal sent to her predator by the jumping gazelle, or the signal the Arabian babbler sends to his congeners as they mob a snake, may be seen as the beginnings of language. Still, we can see in them more than just foreshadowing of codes: we see an indication of good health in the gazelle, and an index of courage in the Arabian babbler. Could we say then that there is language here since information is transmitted, no matter whether such transmission is based in a code? There is a clear need to define the concept of information.

Despite its importance in our lives and our understanding of the world, a clear definition of the concept appears to have so far eluded us. We shall consider several definitions in Chapter 4. For the present, we only say that information modifies the state of whoever receives it. This remark, apparently self-evident, implies that information must exist for a given observer. However, there is no indication here that the observer is to be human. It is enough that the observer is able to decode what interests him/her/it. Furthermore, we shall say that the effect of a piece of information is to *simplify* an aspect of the functioning of the observer. This is intuitively easy to understand. The lion has his choice simplified when he sees the gazelle staging her beautiful leap: he knows that he is not going to set up a chase. The bee about to go foraging receives information from her sister's dance. Her choice of the direction of flight is simplified to the point of determining it. In general, the quantity of information transmitted is measured by the magnitude of the simplification it has caused.

There can be information even when there is no language. The sun does not speak to us to tell us that the day has dawned. Conversely, the languages of nature in which we are interested in this book exist because some entities take the trouble to provide information to other entities able to decode it. If the living world is buzzing with the number of languages surrounding it, it is not merely because of the flow of matter and energy. It is because information plays a fundamental part in the process. If nature *speaks*, it is because information circulating within it favors, in one manner or another, entities transmitting it and those receiving it. The actors who exit the information game cease to exist. As information experts, human beings may be allotted a degree of centrality in the living world. By an accident of evolution, they became experts in a field that serves as the unifying principle for all of life, from society down to the molecule through the ecosystem. The language of human beings is only one very particular form of transmission of information, which they use to improve their social value. Most may not suspect that at each second the trillions of macromolecules that constitute their body are also engaged in the process of exchanging information.

2

Genetic Information

We started out with a view of information in the form that is most intuitive and most familiar to us, that is information in human communication. This notion of information involves a sender and a receiver, as well as a supporting code or language. We saw that this notion could easily be extended to animal communication. Can we go further, and speak of information, language and code in connection with biology in general? Of course we can. A domain of biology in which information plays a leading role, and which deserves a close study in its own right, is genetics. How this field is related to information, language, code and the specific features of that relationship are issues that we will consider in the following.

2.1. A central concept in biology

Molecular biology devotes particular attention to information that is transmitted from generation to generation. The message of heredity is generally carried by an element of DNA. DNA is a linear chain consisting of pairs of nucleotides. The four nucleotides that constitute DNA are designated by the letters A, T, G and C, which stand for the corresponding molecules that are the chemical bases: adenine, thymine, guanine and cytosine. However, DNA does not resemble a string of pearls, in which each base would be one of four possible bases. Instead, it is more like a ladder (see Figure 1.1), in which each rung is a pair of nucleotides. This happens because of the affinities that exist between A and T, and between C and G. These affinities arise from hydrogen bonds that are strong enough to preserve their association, but not strong enough to make that association irreversible. The sequence of nucleotides is made complete by its complement, thus producing the well-known double helix that James Watson and Francis Crick discovered in 1953. The ladder was seen to be twisted so as to appear shaped like a helix. Each nucleotide faces its complement on this ladder – A with T, T with A, C with G, G with C. It is this mirror-like arrangement that allows DNA to replicate itself identically, since each half-ladder (the ladder cut in half along its length) possesses the information that enables it to constitute a complete ladder.

A small portion of DNA is written into a molecule of RNA, which is itself a sequence of nucleotides. RNA has U (for uracil) corresponding to the T in DNA, and, in general, has the form of a single strand, compared to DNA's two complementary strands. Transcription from DNA into RNA is carried out by a set of enzymes using the DNA as a template, and also using the other nucleotides as well as the power generated by the nutrition and the metabolism of the host. Also used in the process is the affinity existing among the bases A, T, C and G in DNA that pair, respectively, with RNA's U, A, G and C. RNA is capable of working directly within a cell, perhaps after undergoing some transformations, and consequently a message in DNA can also appear in RNA. This is particularly observed in the case of ribosomal RNA (rRNA) and transfer RNA (tRNA), both of which will be considered in detail later on. However, at this point, we shall only add that a messenger RNA ("mRNA") would be needed to make possible the synthesis of a new molecule, which is a protein, or, more precisely, a polypeptide sequence.

The transition of a DNA segment to mRNA was initially thought to be a word-for-word transcription process, but the first sequencing of DNA, in the 1980s, brought a surprise: among the eukaryotes (the organisms, including multicellular organisms, whose cells constitute a nucleus), mRNA undergoes changes that in turn modify the message it carries. These changes affect the functions of splicing and editing. This implies that the transition is an act of *interpretation*. In this context, splicing is an operation that removes parts of mRNA prior to translation. These parts, called introns, are present in the genome, but are not used in the process of the synthesis of a protein. The removal of introns is carried out by enzymes, or by one of the introns themselves. A second surprise lay in the discovery that an RNA could fold upon itself, and could take on an enzymatic function. At the same time, it was found that the editing function was relatively rarely performed. Also, upon the completion of mRNA's task, certain nucleotides are replaced by others in a systematic manner. Consequently, the information in its translated form may not necessarily be identical to the original information in the DNA (Watson *et al.* 2008).

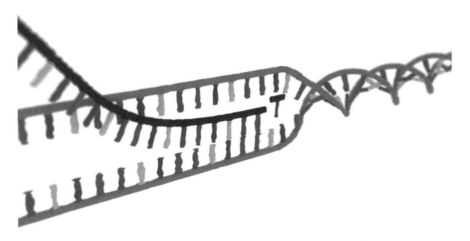

Figure 2.1. *The translation of a DNA molecule into a mRNA molecule (courtesy of DataBase Center for Life Science (DBCLS)). For a color version of this figure, see www.iste.co.uk/gaucherel/information.zip*

The translation of the mRNA in proteins is carried out by a complex machinery that is now relatively well known. It has to do with the translation of information carried by the mRNA in a sequence of amino acids. This mechanism has been studied in detail by molecular biologists (Job and Eberwine 1912; Hajj and Whitehead 2017). We shall only recall here some fundamental elements of it.

At this point, we may add a comment on the similarity between the terminologies of genetics and human language. A segment of DNA is a sequence of *letters* (initials of the nucleotides). The *transcription* of DNA into RNA copies the message letter for letter on to another medium. *Translation* allows transition into another language, that of proteins. The purpose (we shall see later what we mean by that term) is to produce a protein that will generate an action according to its characteristics (form, distribution of electric charges, etc.). There is a *reading system* that reads the message the mRNA carries. The reading is done by *words* consisting of three letters, called *codons*. The sequence of codons, initially carried by DNA, but now carried by mRNA, is a *sentence* that can direct the production of a protein. It is this sentence that we call a *gene*.

The proteins in living beings are made up of 20 or more amino acids. We could imagine (and actually produce) other amino acids, but there will always be these 20 that we encounter in nature. However, for the action of passing from the genetic message to the protein to happen, it is necessary that the codons of the message be read sequentially. The sequence AUGGCGGAA..., for example, is seen by the reading device as the sequence of codons: AUG-GCG-GAA-... Since four different nucleotides exist, only 64 possible codons are corresponding to the 20 acids considered. This correspondence is made possible by transfer RNAs (tRNAs). Some 60 tRNAs are known today, one per codon (some codons do not have corresponding tRNAs: the transcription stops with them). A given tRNA bonds with one of the 20 amino acids, always the same one each time, on the one hand, and is able, on the other hand, to attach itself to its corresponding codon. To do this, the tRNA uses the affinities among its nucleotides and those of the codon: A associates easily with U, and C with G. The tRNAs constitute a dictionary that helps translate the language of the mRNA into the language of the proteins. This dictionary also uses enzymes (called aminoacyl-tRNA transferases) that combine amino acids with tRNAs. Rather than try to describe in detail the precise mechanisms that end up producing a protein from a gene, we shall only say that these enzymes and these tRNAs constitute a system that allows a translation of the message from DNA into proteins.

The sequence of the three nucleotides in a tRNA that binds to the codons of an mRNA is called an anticodon. The anticodon complements the codon reading, for example, CAC to read GUG. At the other extreme, from the side that constructs protein, there is attached an amino acid, always the same for a given anticodon. The preceding anticodon is thus bound to valine, one of the 20 possible amino acids. A complex machinery allows a sequential placing of tRNAs facing their respective codons and amino acids to then assemble the amino acids, and to separate them from their tRNAs. Protein is constructed gradually, linearly, from the first codon to the last.

There are several different tRNAs for certain codons, and it is possible that a particular tRNA is able to translate more than one codon (the pairing of the third base of the codon is not strictly compulsory). Now, there is correspondence between a given anticodon and the amino acid always paired with it, and it is the function of aminoacyl-RNA transferases to ensure this correspondence. The code, physically constituted by these molecules, defines what we call the "genetic code" (the word "code" in the present context connotes "correspondence of all descriptions that enables the transformation of one coded message into another", not the meaning the computer scientist has assigned to the word). It provides, for all possible codons, the corresponding amino acid, for example, for the codon UUU the amino acid phenylalamine.

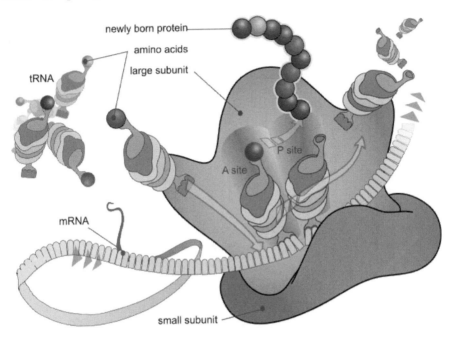

Figure 2.2. *The mRNA molecule and the tRNA molecules are gradually building proteins*

It is easily seen that with the four letters A, U, C and G, which represent the nucleotides of RNA, we can form $4 \times 4 \times 4 = 64$ codons of three letters. Three of these codons (UAA, UAG and UGA) serve as punctuation marks (we could call them "stop" codons), and no tRNA carries (in general) the corresponding anticodon. That leaves 61 codons to represent 20 amino acids. The code is said to have "degenerated", an unfortunate label that might suggest that the code was better before, but actually indicates that several codons specify the same amino acid. The number of codons specifying the same amino acid varies from one (AUG for methionine, which also allows the transcription to start, or UCG for tryptophan) to six (UAA, UUG and CUx for leucine, and AGA, AGG and CGx for arginine, x representing any nucleotide that one may choose) (Lehmann and Libchaber 2008; Watson *et al.* 2008). Thus, it often happens that a change in the third letter of the codon does not change the specific amino acid.

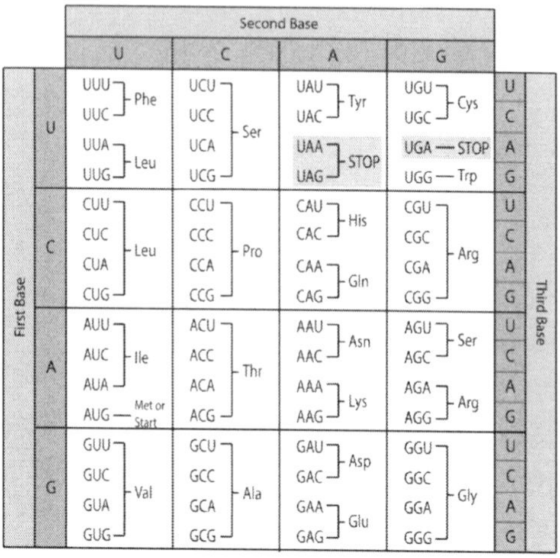

Figure 2.3. *Classification of amino acids according to their constitutive nucleotides and to their order of appearance (courtesy of Sarah Greenwood). For a color version of this figure, see www.iste.co.uk/gaucherel/information.zip*

This code is said to be universal, in the sense that all terrestrial living beings (bacteria, archaea, plants, animals, mushrooms, algae and others) use it with slight variations. Certain minor modifications have already been experimented with: some synthetic genes called "suppressors" correspond to the production of a tRNA capable of binding an AA to a "stop" codon. Researchers are working on wide-ranging modifications harnessing amino acids and nucleotides that do not belong to the kinds currently being used by living forms (Capecchi 1967; Scolnick *et al.* 1968).

Following our analogy between the biological code and human language (Chapter 1), a gene is an informational entity that roughly corresponds to a sentence. It is surrounded by punctuation marks (opening codon, closing codon), and produces an mRNA that, when translated, will lead to the production of a sequence of amino acids (tens to hundreds of them), the sequence of which depends on the sequence of the letters of the gene. However, while the syntax of the genetic language is not fully known, a methionine codon is always what one starts with, and a "stop" codon is always what one ends with. At the present time, we are looking for regularities in the different modifying mechanisms that control the change between the sequence in DNA and the one that appears when translated (Brenner *et al.* 1965; Zhang *et al.* 2005). We are also studying the regularities in many of the genes, parts of which correspond to the domains characteristic of the protein in terms of form, function, etc. It would be interesting to examine these features in greater detail.

Amino acids have two main characteristics: one of them can easily attach itself to another in a linear chain to form proteins, and all combinations of them *a priori* seem possible. A combination of 20 amino acids can produce $20^{200} \approx 10^{260}$ proteins of 200 amino acids, a number that boggles the imagination – the number of atoms in the universe is probably of the order of 10^{80}. Hence, no more than a tiny fraction of that space has been explored by life. Amino acids differ widely in terms of form and electrical charge distributions, and hydrophilicity and hydrophobicity. Consequently, the chain of amino acids cannot arbitrarily fold back upon itself.

It has long been held that a given sequence of amino acids only corresponds to a single folding, a single possible shape. We know, however, that this is not always true, and the matter is still under investigation (Rothemund 2006). The folding of the protein may depend on factors that, in turn, depend on the reading system. There are proteins called "chaperones" that help other proteins fold. Folding may also depend on the environment. For example, metallic ions influence the folding of proteins, and in fact make it possible, as in the case of hemoglobin. Certain proteins are called "autochaperones", and these signify that the first folded shapes play a part in the folding of the proteins formed later. We understand that in such a case an abnormal fold can occur, and this is the explanation currently being accepted for the existence of prions, malformations of folds of a protein of which the sequence is normal, but which is propagated by inducing malignant folds that are fatal to the organism (Prusiner 1991; Miyazawa *et al.* 2012).

The message of DNA, transcribed into mRNA, and then translated into protein, generates a collection of proteins, each one of which has a specific shape. It does this with the help of a mechanism involving, notably, proteins, RNAs and sugars. Its shape is directly responsible for the sort of property that the particular protein possesses, such as attaching itself to a membrane, or crossing it, or attracting one or more other molecules, or putting them in contact, or causing a particular reaction, or producing fibers, or transmitting a signal, or recognizing a form (an antigen), or attaching itself to DNA

(Sjölander 2004; Tuteja and Tuteja 2004). There exists huge possibilities, and these include a wide variety of functions that allow all living beings to exist, perceive, react and adapt themselves to a multiplicity of environmental conditions.

2.2. Epigenetic information

If the information from nucleic acids translated into the language of proteins has the capacity to do all the things we have just enumerated, the proteins themselves, as carriers of information, do not carry "messages" in the sense that we have assigned to the word. The information contained in proteins is not a message in that it cannot be copied or translated. Only nucleic acids for which there are possibilities of transcription in the two directions (DNA→RNA and RNA→DNA), and a possibility of replication (DNA→DNA), carry information that can be replicated.

Research for most molecular biologists today consists of trying to discover how a genome produces an organism. This standpoint has drawn criticism. To cite one example, in his *The Triple Helix,* Richard Lewontin finds fault with the thinking that this approach represents ("molecular biologists do not usually call attention to this ignorance about the determination of protein structure but instead repeat the mantra that DNA makes proteins"). Actually, it is not the genome that produces an organism, but an assemblage of information contained within the message– decoder–environment (MDE) triad, described earlier (see the Introduction). More precisely, it is the organism, when placed in its environment (an environment that it contributed to build), that reads the message that produces the proteins that produce a copy of the genome.

The message, which in the present context happens to be the genome, is only a single element of the assemblage: each individual gene may be read to some degree at a particular instant, at a particular point, in a particular part of the organism. The types of control that such an action implies are the responsibility of the organism. It has at its disposal many mechanisms that make possible the expression of each gene. It can produce hormones that activate the reading of certain genes, and inhibit the reading of others. It can even modify DNA chemically (Evans and Evans 1970; Rana and Ankri 2016). A small structure, made up of one atom of carbon and three of hydrogen (called methyl), constitutes a sort of marker that could be pasted almost anywhere on the genome. This methylation process can be used to some degree to read the gene "tagged" in this fashion. Even more importantly, the enzymes that can copy DNA can choose whether or not to reproduce the methylation in the copy. If they do, epigenetic modification is transmitted to the progeny.

We recall that the gene, once it is transcribed in RNA, can undergo changes. It is often spliced (parts of it, called "introns", have been removed before translation) and edited (nucleotides, always the same, have been replaced by others). These changes may constitute a mechanism possessing remarkable flexibility. Splicing of another type occurs when a single gene can see an intron (or a part of an intron) removed, or retained, depending upon the case in point. The presence of the corresponding part of the protein will then be open to change after translation. We observe even cases in which alternative splicing leads to a change in the size of the reading frame through a change in the size of the part removed by a number that is not a multiple of 3, and modifying all the codons downstream (Black 2003; Zahler et al. 2003). We see that a gene can take different "meanings" depending on how it is read, much as certain phrases in our language can receive different interpretations depending on the tone in which they are said, or their written punctuation or oral rhythm.

Genes do not express themselves. They are read and interpreted by the reading system, the organism. Just as a cookery book does not prepare a dish, the genome only provides instructions while it is the organism that acts. For its part, the organism possesses information that would have been of little interest by itself if there were no genome to be read. This information, called "epigenetic", can also be transmitted under certain conditions.

An early model of the stability of epigenetic information was the one proposed in the 1960s, and given the name "flow balance" (Baum et al. 2014; Dorri et al. 2016). Assume two genes A and B, each producing a gene that can suppress the other. In other words, A's protein inhibits the expression of B and vice versa. If there is no disturbance to the system during reproduction, the descendants of the cell that contain protein A will continue to let gene A be expressed while preventing gene B from being expressed. The "read A, and not B" information is thus inherited. Suppose now that the product of gene B is introduced massively into the environment of the cell. This will have the effect of inhibiting the expression of A. Not expressed up to this point, gene B is now expressed, and this inhibits the expression of A. We can see that the cells and their descendants are going to express gene B, and not gene A, if the environment does not contain anything to affect this system. There is no genetic difference between the starting cells that express A, and not B, and the end cells that express B, and not A. The two types share the same genome. They share the same environment. The difference between them is *epigenetic*.

Epigenetic information is an essential element of the MDE set, while it is not clear that it should receive the status of a message. Unlike genetic information, epigenetic information appears not to result from a systematic combination of simpler elements. Its status in biology is very much in progress (Danchin *et al.* 2011a; Francis 2011). Disdained in the early days of genetics, but defended by the academic C. H. Waddington, epigenetic information was later somewhat forgotten. It does smell a little bit of sulfur with a touch of Lamarckism. The concept received some attention from biologists early in the 21st Century, and it is particularly important to clarify it. We propose the view that epigenetic information corresponds to the information contained in the reading system, with all its concomitant merits, limitations and constraints.

If we may use a simile, epigenetic information allows one to interpret the genome, much as a musician interprets a musical composition. We also recognize that there could be differences between two interpretations. There is the musical score, and there is the music actually played. We might hear a music lover say he/she likes a piece performed in such and such a style, to the exclusion of other styles, and with a particular quality of interpretation. While this may be so, there is still another factor to be taken into account: the environment. Some music lovers know this feeling. For reasons that we do not know, apart from the quality of the music and the performer, something produces a magical moment. A stillness in the chamber, a mood … In contrast, the best of performers playing a masterpiece would not stand a chance with a drill in action!

2.3. The environment

With the genome and the organism, we have two pieces of Lewontin's triple helix. Let us add the third, and we can then go on to develop a story … an evolutionist one, no doubt. All organisms, all living beings, interpret information, but always in a given context. The environment constitutes one part essentially external to the organism. Whether there is heating or cooling of the climate, or humidity undergoes change, or the resources grow or shrink, or change nature, or neighbors become more aggressive, the organism will undergo an appropriate change in its functioning. We should not forget that the organism also influences its environment. It constructs it partially and can, in most cases, choose it.

The genetic and epigenetic assemblage cannot construct an organism in the absence of a pre-existing environment that provides the physicochemical conditions and the resources which make up the living being. This fact is overlooked in most teaching or explanation of genetics. Wilhelm Johannsen, in 1909, introduced to the community of biologists the concepts of genotype and phenotype. These terms now appear unfortunate. They date back to the typological view that had long prevailed in biology. A type was supposed to be predefined (by the Creator until the 19th Century, and later by the genes), and to decide what the individual concerned is going to be like owing to the "circumstances" of the environment. With Johannsen it seemed that the notion of type was no longer applied to the species, but to the genome (this explains the origin of the word "genotype"). This idea of a genetic predefinition only is totally false. The notion as developed by Johannsen was more opulent (Johannsen 1911). The individual is co-produced by his/her genome (his/her genotype) and his/her environment. There is nothing that is determined by the genes or qualified by the environment. There is no one part that is more different from either of the other two. Each living being is the result of a complete interaction between its genome and its environment: each living being is determined 100% by biology and 100% by the environment.

Geneticists sometimes give measures of what they call in their jargon the part of genetics and the part of the environment in the determination of a characteristic. The part of genetics is called "heritability". What does this property mean for a given characteristic such as skin color, or IQ or weight that can be measured? Before we can offer an answer, we must clarify that this is a statistical measure of how much of the *variation* in the characteristics is due to variations in the genes, and how much to variations in the environment, in a given population within a given range of environments. In other words, what proportion of characteristics inherited from parents can be attributed to genes, and, separately, to variations in the environment? This question has diverse and sometimes perverse consequences. Epigenetic information, depending on whether it is inherited down to the generations or not, will therefore count with the genetic or the environmental. We might add that the environmental part that the organism builds around it may be counted as genetic.

Which of the two factors has more impact on a particular characteristic? This is a bit like someone asking the winner of a motorcycle race, "What part did the rider play, and what part did the engine play in the victory?" The rider may answer: "50/50". Is he implying that without the motorcycle his chances of winning the race would have been halved? And conversely for the motorcycle without him? Well, there is some truth in what the statement implies, but not necessarily in the number.

In a lit electric bulb, what is the measurable role of the bulb and what is the measurable role of the electric current in the emission of light? Clearly, the presence of each is absolutely necessary. Now, if we come to a house in which some bulbs light up and others do not, we can easily say what proportion of bulbs is defective, and in what proportion the current does not flow. We can then determine the part played by the bulbs, and the part played by the current, in the lighting conditions in the house. Of course, the figure we arrive at will only be valid for the particular house we have considered, and says nothing about electric supply in general. These two analogies also apply to attempts to distinguish between the roles played by biology and the environment in natural phenomena.

Now what about the motorcycle and the rider? We will change the scenario a bit. A competition they have in the equestrian world might be interesting in this context. Four riders take part in an obstacle race, each on his or her own horse. They change their mounts after each run. This means that each of the four horses and each of the four riders will have taken turns with the others. In this case, we can determine the relative part of the rider and the horse in the win. Suppose it is one particular rider that always wins, never mind which horse he rides. We can then say that it is the rider who decides the result. Conversely, if it is a particular horse that always wins, regardless of who rides him, we could say that it is the horse that decides the result. We can see intuitively in such a situation, regardless of the results, that we can separate the part the rider has played in the win from the part the horse has played, with a single interaction. This was clearly what the motorcyclist wished to indicate. We thus note two points. One, what we are considering is the rank, a difference between results, not the phenomenon itself (the contest involving a human–equine pair). Two, the result is contingent: it is only valid for this particular race, on this particular day, with a particular horse and rider team. We might lay a bet that, if one of us (presumably not equestrian champions) were to take part in such a contest, we might heighten the influence of the rider in the result – by consistently failing to win!

We shall return to the subject of heredity and the environment. "Heritability", as we have said earlier, is the part of genetics in the manifestation of particular traits in an organism. Now, what does the term stand for? For those familiar with statistics, heritability is the ratio of genetic variance to total variance. To clarify this definition without going into a mass of detail, consider the variation that we might observe in a population, say a variety of beans (with due respect to Johannssen). In this case, the variation may be in size. We might measure the size of individual beans in the crop, and try to relate it to the size of their "parents". Now, beans, like peas and wheat, being autogamous (self-fertilizing), each individual has the same individual as father and mother. Otherwise, it is a little complicated, but we proceed regardless.

In the closing years of the 19th Century, Francis Galton, a cousin of Charles Darwin, and founder of eugenics and biometry, carried out experiments on peas to test this hypothesis. Finding that descendants of extreme individuals had a tendency to approach the mean, compared to their parents, he spoke of *regression* (the heredity of geniuses was what interested him). The word has remained in statistics to designate the law (or the curve) that governs the relationship between one variable and another dependent variable (in this case, the size of the parent and the size of the descendant). Later, Johannsen had the idea of repeating the experiment with seven generations, separating within each successive pair of generations the largest beans from the smallest in the progeny (Johannsen 1911). He found, like Galton, that in the first generation, descendants of the largest were larger than the mean, but smaller than their parent, and, symmetrically, the descendants of the smallest were smaller than the mean, but larger than their parent. However, the pattern did not persist in succeeding generations. Whether he chose the largest or the smallest, the beans from the smallest at the beginning produced descendants of a constant mean size and the same as that for the largest beans. The mean size of the descendants from the largest beans at the beginning remained greater than that of the descendants of the smallest at the beginning.

Johannsen had deduced in 1906 that a variation in the starting population was transmitted on the basis of his finding that descendants of the largest were on average larger than descendants of the smallest. This variation did not, however, continue in succeeding generations in the two populations, one consisting of the largest beans, the other of the smallest. Clearly, part of the variation is not transmissible. The variation of the beans chosen at the beginning of the experiment consisted of two types: one part transmissible the other non-transmissible. The transmissible part of variation is considered to represent the variation due to the diversity from genotypes, and the other part that is attributable to the environment.

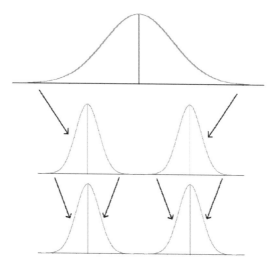

Figure 2.4. *Trait distributions from the parents (up) to offsprings (bottom). In case of the distribution of sizes in a population, we observe a mean-reversion in descendant distributions*

Some outstanding statisticians, R. A. Fisher in particular, developed this model, and were able to define the genetic part of the variation and its non-genetic part, and then break the different parts down into subcategories (Fisher 1915, 1918). The important thing is to understand that it is not the cause of the size of the bean that is the focus of study here, but the cause of the *variations* in size within the sample chosen. The variance thus obtained is only valid for this population and in this range of environments. Change the range of environments, and/or the genetic composition of the population, and everything will then change–the total variance, the genetic part of the environment. If we find, for example, that in the sample of beans at the start of Johannsen's study, the genetic part is 60%, this result is only valid for this lot of beans in this particular field. From the second generation onwards, for each of the two classes that he made on the basis of size, the genetic part in the variation he observed was nil: whether he chose descendants of the largest or those of the smallest, the offspring were alike. All of the variation was therefore due to the environment. Actually, starting with a single bean, all the descendants were genetically similar, and any variation then could only have come from the environment.

Finally, the geneticist's study of characteristics is restricted to defining how a range of diverse genotypes within a range of environments produces a range of values for a characteristic, and to differentiating variations in those characteristics due to genetic (transmissible) variations from those due to environmental (non-transmissible) variations. We are not interested in a particular fundamental trait, but in one contingent measure of the separation between the transmissible and the non-transmissible in a designated sample in a given setting. We believe that this insight might well be something that will contribute to improving milk production capacity in French dairy livestock, for example. If we find the heritability (the proportion of genetic variation in the total variation) to be 23%, this will tell us nothing about the biological mechanisms of milk production. On the other hand, it may suggest that more effort should be directed toward the environment of the cattle than to their artificial selection. If we were to shift our focus to the Sahel (the semiarid region stretching from Senegal to the Sudan), we would have to start all over again. A hundred years since the genotype was first defined, heritability values are still presented to laypeople as having a general value. Heritability is still often attributed to the characteristic, while it is only valid for the variations in the characteristics, and only within the population under study, in the given environment.

Worse, one may use these experiments to define a "genotypic value" of a characteristic that is only the mean of the values taken by the assemblage of individuals possessing the genotype over the range of the settings tested. This notion is very misleading. It creates the impression that the genotype determines a value and that the environment modulates it. It does nothing of the sort. The genotype, we must repeat, determines nothing without the environment, and the value found for a genotype evidently depends on the range of environments over which it is tested. But, while these values manipulated by the experts do not present a problem, they constitute a catastrophic instance of disinformation, particularly for the level of biology students better trained to handle pipettes than they are to handle statistical concepts.

2.4. Information: from replication to reproduction

The information contained within a message, and decoded by the reading system in a given environment, produces an effect on the physical world. It has one other property, the power of being copied. A copy thus produced can itself interact with a reading system, and can be copied as often as desired. The reproduction process consists of reconstituting the message in a suitable medium. It is fascinating to contemplate the variety of copying methods that man has invented. From monk-copyists to information systems using photocopiers that utilize static electricity or magnetophones that use the permanence of magnetic devices, there is an enormous array of physicochemical properties at work to help the process forward.

In comparison, the copying of genetic information is a monotonous process. Its working is remarkably homogeneous across the entire living world. The nucleotides pair off in accordance with the Watson–Crick laws: the A–T and G–C base pairs that allow an assemblage of enzymes to copy the DNA molecule from the beginning to the end. The base pairing works correctly except in a certain proportion of cases (of the order of 10^{-8}) which, on the scale of genomes of several millions (or rather billions) of nucleotides, is far from negligible. If we take into account the fact that numerous environmental factors (chemical such as mutagens, physical such as the sun's rays) can substantially increase this rate, we can see that a DNA copy can give rise to errors. An accumulation of errors can rapidly compromise the integrity of the genetic information of living beings whose genome is of substantial size, if those organisms did not have in place correction systems *a posteriori*. However, there are several systems that can spot and fix the anomalies after replication. Errors that remain are mutations. Their frequency can be of an order of 10^{-9} per nucleotide per year in the case of mammals. Notice that the repair mechanisms are made up of enzymes whose structure is encoded in the genome, implying that these mechanisms can themselves suffer damage through mutations. Indeed, we know of many mutations that have caused mutations of the entire genome to increase by a factor of 10, 100, or even 1,000 (Pray 2008; Tomasetti *et al.* 2017). Now, while a copying error almost always produces a negative effect, as in the case of information transmitted by human languages, there are some mutations that are beneficial.

Biological systems possess a particular property, which is that the MDE assemblage in their case works in such a way that it can reproduce itself.

This is an extraordinary property that can, for example, explain the origin of all living beings. The information contained in the genome allows the reading system (and the epigenetic information that it contains) to produce not only new copies of the message *but also new reading systems*, all within an environment that could perhaps be going through change. It is like if the cook-and-cookery-book analogy we used before now produces not only the dish, but also a well-off chef with a brand new cookery book. The information in the message multiplies along with the reading system itself. But, as we shall see, this can change over time, because the entire MDE assemblage changes and evolves under the action of several forces. The evolution, which brought us to life, is basically a product of information.

2.5. Mutation and selection

Biological systems are self-reproducing, or, from a logical point of view, belong to systems called self-referential. These are of a circular-causality kind, or at least of a spiral-causality kind: the familiar chicken-or-egg paradox resembles a circle, if we overlook the time span between the instant the egg brings forth the chicken and when the chicken lays the egg. If one were to take that time span into account, the circle would turn into a spiral. We can represent the line of generations in the form of a cycle in which parents produce descendants who themselves become parents. This cycle becomes a spiral when we add the time dimension (viewed from its extremity, a cylindrical spiral appears like a circle). Early 20th-Century information experts, such as Alan Turing, who laid the foundations of information science, were not wrong when they recognized this fascinating aspect of such self-reproducing systems.

Self-reproducing systems are capable of evolving spontaneously if two conditions are met: the first, the message is one that can vary, with the variations being transmissible, as in the case of the genome and human messages, and the second, the message and its reading system are able to reproduce themselves with such variations as their working may require. We might say that these systems are subject to selection. This is certainly the case with cookery book recipes, the good ones being copied and used more frequently than those that are not so good, and the genomes, those producing efficient reading systems being copied more frequently than those that do not.

Darwin was the first to understand that natural selection is linked to differential reproduction: not all individuals contribute equally to the succeeding generation. Actually, it is the MDE assemblage that reproduces itself, as we have just seen. Selection results from a differential reproduction of different MDE systems. Darwin discovered that some MDE systems are more efficient than others in terms of reproduction, and that they alone last over a course of time. The message, here the genome, contains the information that allows the reading system (here the living being) to produce, with varying degrees of efficiency, copies of the genome and new living beings in the environment considered. All genomes that are capable of producing reading systems more efficient than the average, in terms of the acquisition of resources, will see their representation in the existing assemblage of genomes increase.

If there were to be a process that could accommodate diversity in messages, this race in reproduction would be unending, and after a large enough number of repetitions there would only be left the messages that would allow the production or reproduction of reading systems as well adapted as possible to the current environment. The message becomes something of an end in itself, producing reading systems that replicate the best available. This is not to say that the message is in itself a thought, or a conscious act, or a feeling, but simply that, out of a vast collection of possibilities, only those that maximize their reproduction within given constraints, and in particular in environmental fluctuations, survive. The reading systems thus produced are optimized for the reproduction of the message and the production of other reading systems that are their descendants. The mutation that creates the variation and the selection that only preserves the messages inducing the existence of the most efficient MDE systems (in the current conditions, of course) then creates dynamic conditions optimizing the assemblage for maximal reproduction.

This presentation is largely based on the classical Darwinist theory of evolution. It offers an explanation of the working and diversification of living beings. It explains why living beings are optimized for the reproduction of genes, and by what process they are adapted to the different environments that they may colonize for long periods (Darwin 1859, retrieved October 24, 2008). It presents living beings as artifices "invented" by genes in order to reproduce themselves, some of which may be found satisfactory, others inadequate, still others simplistic. This "genocentrist" point of view has at least the merit that it provides a conceptual framework from which to ask other questions. It does not respond to all of them, however. If it explains why there are living beings adapted to the environment, it says almost nothing in answer to the questions "Why these beings?" or "Why these adaptations?" Contingency, the collection of random events that led to the beings that we observe, remains an open question.

The genocentrist perspective focuses on the information in the message, and has little to do with information of an epigenetic or environmental nature. Now, two elements of the MDE set, namely the decoder (including the epigenetic) and the environment, influence the game of selection. According to how the epigenetic and the environmental factors influence the genetic expression, the working of the organism will vary in efficiency in terms of the reproduction of genetic information (Danchin *et al.* 2011a). This has important implications.

First, the genetic information will have been selected in order to influence the epigenetic and the environmental factors so as to maximize its reproduction. Since the organism consists of elements that are themselves constituted of elements of information from the genome, we may accept the idea that the genome controls all that happens in the organism. At the same time, since genetic information only expresses itself through the epigenetic prism, we may also imagine that epigenetic information enjoys a certain degree of autonomy. As for the environment, we know that the organism can control one part of it: homoeothermy (control by an organism of its internal temperature) and viviparity are obvious instances. However, there are several reasons we cannot say that organisms control their entire environment. For one thing, some elements of the environment remain outside the bounds of influence of the organism. For another, some of the actions of the organism do have adverse effects, from its point of view, on the environment, for example, bacteria, plants and animals that feed on the resources, and thus tend to deplete their environment. Some such actions may impact the organism's fellow beings, while it remains untouched itself, never mind that it was responsible for that damage in the first place! We could point to several instances of this happening in the human species (MEA 2005; retrieved August 7, 2014). The actions of the kind described cannot give rise to a selection as they do not create differences between different messages in terms of information reproduction.

Second, genetic information and epigenetic information probably coevolved. Epigenetic information can survive for several generations, and the selection process for genetic information may also be reproduced with epigenetic information. This is where our present knowledge of the subject rests. For how many generations does epigenetic information remain autonomous? We do not at this stage have an answer to the question. It is possible that the epigenetic information that the components of the organism constantly produce from genetic information is subject to change, and after a large enough number of generations the genetic part alone may survive. Genetic information is hard coded in a particularly stable molecule, that is the DNA. The rest seems to possess little capacity to last, while we must admit, however, that we cannot at the present time be certain that this is so. We could also imagine that, in general, it is in fact genetic information that offers real assurance for the system's integrity over time. However, at some points in time an epigenetic upheaval may occur, causing changes in the conditions, and producing a sustainable new form and expression of the genome. Once this transition has taken place, the selection with the genome can, at least in some cases, lead the genetic information to keep this new state going (Francis 2011). The original epigenetic modification ends up being written into the genes. This is the concept of assimilation that Conrad Hal Waddington proposed in the 1950s, and forms the basis of the belief that teosinte was the wild ancestor of modern maize.

2.6. The story of the message: phylogeny and coalescence

The reading of the genome by the living being that carries it results in replicating the MDE system, while the human being can create a new message without leaving a pre-existing message. This represents a major difference between the biological message constituting the genome and the message woken or written by a human being. Of course, no one can by himself ordinarily invent a complex message. When we speak or write, we are borrowing (without necessarily being conscious of the fact) numerous elements from messages that we had heard or read earlier. However, unlike what happens in the case of genes, an important portion of the messages that we send are not true copies of those that we received. Some of our messages may of course be true copies, such as the words of St John quoted at the beginning of this book. Richard Dawkins conceptualized the notion of the *meme* to describe elements of culture or behavioral systems that human beings replicate through communication (Chapter 1). Copied information files are exact copies, much like what can be said about the genes. This is not an absolute rule, however. While every portion of a genetic message is always a direct copy of a pre-existing message, there need not be a similar direct connection between a new human message and one or more old messages of which the new might have been as close a copy as possible. The human brain produces a wide variety of messages, more diverse than those produced by mutation, even if one were to add gender to the brew. A consequence of this is that, while all of the diversity of the genetic messages has its origin in the errors in the copies, that is the mutations, they clearly play a minor role in the evolution of the messages that we human beings exchange among ourselves.

Genetic information is not produced by the epigenetic system. It is copied, certainly, with its errors, but without being an "invention" by the system other than by chance. There is no "spontaneous" generation of genetic information. One consequence of this is that a given portion of the genomic sequence descends without ambiguity from a sequence of the preceding generation of which it is a copy. The gender aspect inevitably tends to complicate matters a bit, owing to the fact that the genomes mix with each generation, but we may, nevertheless, segment all genomes in groups such that each of their members has descended from a given genome, and only from that genome. We can in theory trace the lineage of all the genomes and of all the individuals to whom they belong. This genealogy of genomes offers a field for some really active research (Hein *et al.* 2005; Arenas and Posada 2014). One of the surprising discoveries made in the domain was the phenomenon of coalescence.

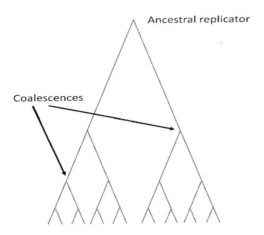

Figure 2.5. *Genealogy of the genetic information highlighting coalescent events*

Each element of information in the genetic message may leave a copy of itself in one or several, or none, of the models from one generation to another. Bearing in mind that the space in which we are interested necessarily has a finite population, in other words a finite number of individual carriers of information, we see that the number of independent genomes is finite. The lineages that we can define from the genealogical tree of the elements of information of the genetic message "coalesce". The following instance will clarify the point. Consider a given portion of the genome of a particular individual, named (let us say) Gregory. Choose, for instance, the gene that encodes for the α hemoglobin chain. This gene is a copy of the same gene that one of his parents had, which in turn he/she had inherited from one of his/her parents, and so on. We can trace the genealogy of this gene through the genealogy of Gregory, or rather through one of the multiple lineages that constitute his genealogy. We shall do something similar with the gene of Charles, another hypothetical individual. We know that we will find a moment in the past where the two lineages meet. They coalesce into a single entity. One of the ancestors, common to Gregory and Charles, had carried the gene of which the genes of Gregory and Charles are copies.

Could it be that, without being aware of it, Gregory and Charles are related? Yes, of course, they are, and here is how. All individuals in a population are related. To show this is so, all we need to do is calculate how many ancestors each of the two had. Each had two parents, $2^2 = 4$ grandparents, $2^3 = 8$ great-grandparents, ... 2^n ancestors going back n generations. If we go back far enough, we shall have an immensely large number, and all the individuals belonging to that particular period of time were probably ancestors of Gregory and Charles, provided that they left behind some descendants. To fix the idea better, let us go back to the time of Charlemagne, that is 12 centuries ago. Taking a generation to mean 24 years, the period comprises roughly 50 generations, and we get $2^{50} \approx 10^{15}$, or about one million billion ancestors just for Gregory, and so for Charles, just as for all of us. There were not as many people then as there are now, and, clearly, some individuals of the time were several times (millions of times, possibly) the ancestors of all of us. We have the same ancestors! We shall see a little later why, despite this, we are all different.

If we were now to have a third man in the frame, say John, drawn from the same population as Gregory's and Charles', we will arrive at a similar result, and Gregory and Charles and now John can point to a common, shared ancestor, if they travel far enough backwards in time. The coalescence phenomenon that this instance represents exists for every individual who belongs to the same population as his/her forebears. As individuals disappear, the principle of coalescence continues to work for those that survive through the segments of the genome that are passed from generation to generation. We may call these segments genes for convenience. For any portion of the genome, we may say that all current copies in the relevant population are descended from the same master copy.

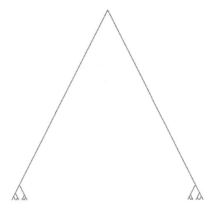

Figure 2.6. *Genealogy of the genetic information with recent coalescence events and from a distant master copy*

Two major mechanisms prevent coalescence. The first is of no particular interest to us. It has to do with the case in which natural selection actively sustains two or more forms of the gene or of the portion of the genome being considered, such as chromosomes. The second is very general. This is the case in which a population breaks up into two parts that no longer exchange genetic information. If one were to trace the history of two genes from that point on, each belonging to one of the two isolated populations, it would become clear that the fact of coalescence could only have occurred before the separation of the two populations.

Now, information transmitted along the branches of the tree of coalescence, as we have seen, is liable to change through mutations. Some of these mutations will modify the message in such a way as to influence the resulting organism, and will consequently modify its potentialities. They then become subject to the selection process, which will eliminate them if the organism's powers of survival and reproduction are diminished, which is most likely to be the case. The mutations will in fact turn out to be for the better, since, by a relatively remote chance, they may improve the individual's performance, this last being seen in terms of a capacity to reproduce the genetic message. Now, a very large proportion of mutations has no effect on the descendant produced, or has no influence on the descendant's ability to reproduce (Kimura 1983). In particular, such "neutral" mutations can take place in non-transcribed areas of the genome, or change a codon in a way that does not change the encoded amino acid. A neutral mutation occurring in a lineage will happen on the assemblage of the branches of the tree of coalescence downstream.

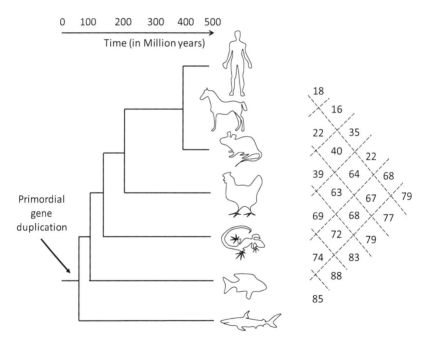

Figure 2.7 *Phylogeny of some animal groups (left) with their distances (right) according to the α and β chains of hemoglobin*

A consequence of this fact is that if we were to examine two copies of even one portion of the genome in two living individuals that are not located at the extremity of the tree of coalescence, we would find that the further away they are from the zero point on the time scale, the more they differ. Specifically, the greater their distance from the zero point, the greater the length of their vertical limbs. This characteristic connects the tree of coalescence to the phylogenetic tree of species, first drawn by Darwin in 1859.

The history of species and the history of their genes run together. This became known in the 1970s, when the first protein sequencing that was carried out showed that the number of differences (shown in the grid on the right of the illustration) between two proteins (here in the α hemoglobin chain) belonging to two current species were directly proportional to their distance in the phylogenetic tree, the tree representing the descent of species, that drew on data from comparative anatomy and paleontology (Darwin 1859; retrieved October 24, 2008; Letunic and Bork 2007). Similar results were found for different genes and for different DNA sequences. There was talk of a molecular clock because neutral mutations were thought to grow proportionately with time. While this clock is admittedly far from perfect, it is thanks to it that we are able today to reconstruct the history of living forms with some precision.

The discovery of genetic coalescence greatly modified how evolutionary geneticists viewed the evolution of living beings. The branches of the tree, which were initially thought to symbolize a chain each link of which was a group of individuals, became carriers of *information*. Following this analogy, what flows through the branches of the tree is genetic (and perhaps epigenetic) information that is copied, not without errors after selection, from generation to generation.

A curious change in perspective takes place in this scenario. In the context of ordinary conditions, individuals are physical entities, concrete and palpable. The genetic information (and epigenetic information, on which we shall have more to say) that they pass on to their descendants must appear abstract and immaterial in comparison. However, if we go back a few hundred million years, the picture we see is quite different. Individuals become so transitory, and their lives so short, that they seem to vanish and are lost to view. What has remained, the phylogeny, is exclusively information that passes through the lineages, seemingly without noticing them. Clearly, at this point, it is information that is singled out for attention. Organisms are only transitory reading systems that this information has gradually built in its crazy, blind race for reproduction. There remains the task of determining the possible autonomous, constant element of epigenetic information at this scale.

2.7. *The point of view of the reading system*

As living beings, human beings initially tried to understand the living world by centering their attention on other living beings. This was quite natural. Biology has essentially centered on the reading system, the organism, the living being. From the naturalistic approach to physiology and its molecular version, biochemistry, the different domains of biology have not stopped raving about the remarkable functional organization of these systems. When the will of a creator stopped being offered as the explanation of their apparent perfection, natural selection took over. However, the topic of natural selection remains something of a riddle pending final recognition of information as a full participant in the processes of the living world.

From the time, in the 1880s, when August Weismann convinced his contemporaries that there was no hereditary aspect to acquired characteristics (we have seen that this notion is less true in the case of epigenetics than one might like to believe), it should have become clear that heritable information passed through individuals without having been produced by them, and that consequently it alone could be selected, the organisms only playing the role of temporary mechanisms charged with reproducing that information. It is noteworthy that a whole century was to pass before Weismann's successors expressed this view of things. Still, the idea of information was hinted at by Weismann when he supposedly used an explicit metaphor in this context comparing the way the somatic cells (cells in the body that do not play a role in reproduction) influence the germ line (the gametes, the cells that reproduce) to the way a telegraphic message that moved from the sender in one language and arrived at its destination in another (Weismann 1868, 1887).

If he did indeed express the idea, it was not assimilated fully. It is astonishing how organismic bias led us to deny information its rightful permanent place. A ready-to-hand example of this is how questions about the phylogenies of species are asked. A typical form a question takes is: "What is good phylogeny?" A legitimate question, of course, but not legitimate under all conditions. In what cases does true phylogeny of species exist? This would require a cohesive group of individuals, ancestor species, split into two groups, both also cohesive, that is only reproducing between themselves. In this case, the genealogy of the genes, obtained with statistical processing, will reflect the history of these groups. However, the actual situation may be much less simple. This will be so for example if genetically distinct groups are differentiated while preserving genetic exchanges for only a portion of the genome, and the separation takes place for this portion much later. When should we date the separation? Some parts of the genome will have one response, other parts will have another. Which of these would be the right one?

The question is not relevant. Still it is hotly debated and defended. During a colloquium in the early 21st Century on phylogeny, a participant spoke of "the evolutionary history of organisms". He may well have been trying to find portions of the genome in the jumble of evolutionary histories. The expression "evolutionary history of organisms" could plunge us into an abyss of thought. What might he have meant by that phrase? Evolutionary history of every one of us? Being organisms, our history begins from the moment of our conception. That moment happened to be when a sperm fertilized an ovum, and the two together produced an egg. The egg possesses a certain genetic constitution, and inherits certain epigenetic determinants. It also occurs in a particular environment. It develops on this basis to produce the organism that we are. Our future, in a manner of speaking, is foreseeable. We will disappear one day. There is no evolutionary history there.

When one speaks of the evolutionary history of organisms, one probably has in mind the genealogy of individuals. However, as we have seen, such a genealogy, owing to its exponential nature, includes everyone but means little else. If we were to analyze the genome of one of our ancestors of some tens of generations ago, we would find in a vast majority of cases that there is strictly nothing that we have inherited. Mendelian laws of heredity lay down that the descendant receives from his/her parent only half of his/her genome. We have therefore only received a quarter of the genomes of our grandparents, an eighth of the genome of our great-grandparents, and a 2^{-n}th of the genome of our ancestor of n generations ago. An ancestor who lived around the year 800, that is some 50 generations ago, has passed on to us averagely 2^{-50} of his/her genome, that is 10^{-15}, that is virtually nothing. The fact that each individual alive at the time is several times our ancestor does seem to add an element of complication to the scene, but the conclusion remains the same for any ancestor randomly picked. This should explain why, while having common ancestors, we still differ from one another. We possess a unique sample of genes taken from the genome pool of the individuals that have given us birth. Under these circumstances, does it make sense to speak of an evolutionary history of organisms, viewed as an assemblage of ancestral lineages? Would it not be more pertinent to focus on the evolutionary history of genetic information that has real stability in time?

Our genes do have an evolutionary history. They come from a distant past, shaped under the action of diverse forces such as mutation, selection and genetic drift; we share them with many contemporary individuals; they will survive us through descendants who now carry them (Gouyon *et al.* 1997). Information alone has the quality of perpetuity. It is information that is passed down, that defines the priorities (its own reproduction) and transgenerational resemblance. The different parts of the genome of one particular species do not share a common history. There can only be a phylogeny of a given species if several different phylogenies coexist within it. The true phylogeny is that of the genes, or more precisely, the phylogeny of parts of the genome. What we imagine for organisms is only an attempt on our part, poor reading systems really, to reclaim the power of the message.

2.8. We cannot see the wood for the trees

It is a complicated task to represent in the form of a tree the genealogy of species (phylogeny). Lamarck apparently proposed dots to represent the seeds of independent evolutionary trees for plants and animals. The first proper phylogenic tree appeared in Darwin's work, *On the Origin of Species*. Darwin's tree is abstract and is intended to apply to all forms of life and at all scales.

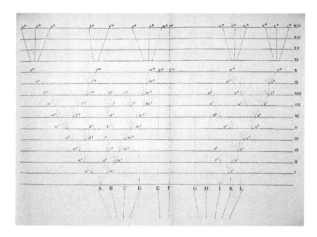

Figure 2.8. *The famous phylogenic tree drawn in Darwin's book on origin of species*

Different versions of the tree have appeared since the 1850s. In their more recent forms, they do not explain the process, but place the species correctly on the tree. Ernst Haeckel was one of the principal authors that got involved in the experiment. While Darwin had taken great care to explain the fact that all current species are at the same evolutionary level, we can see that Haeckel could not help putting Man alone at the top of the tree, an error that has persisted down to this day.

The question of what the branches of the tree stand for is, as we have seen, a complicated epistemological question. We can see there organisms that procreate, the sorts of ideal folk of the species concerned, or of information. The trees may be meant to trace the evolutionary history of species or simply to designate a hierarchical order of their classification. Many authors believe that the last two points ought to be considered equivalent, while some of them would like to break free from one or the other.

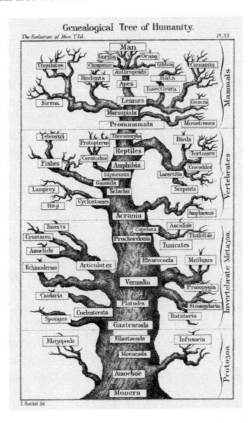

Figure 2.9. *The famous phylogenic tree drawn in Haeckel's book*

It is still the case that this representation remains in circulation, and has kept alive the ambiguity through the entity that is evolving, is passing down, and is selected. The production of several such trees of the living forms has become part of the basic activities of biology laboratories. The trees are produced mainly by a study of the coalescence of genetic information (Hein *et al.* 2005). We have underlined the importance of serious reflection on what coalescence is and what phylogeny is. Theory is here lagging behind practice. A way needs to be found to determine if the concept of species should be left alone, or whether it should be made to evolve into something more information orientated. We shall return to this point later.

Meanwhile, the ongoing study of the history of species, starting with the history of genetic information, has recorded a big surprise. It used to be believed earlier that there were only two major types of living being: the eukaryotes and the prokaryotes. The eukaryotes, the category to which we human beings belong, are beings consisting of a single cell (a paramecium is an example) or of several cells containing a kernel (such as happens in the case of humans). The chromosomes, carriers of genetic information, reside in the kernel. The kernel itself is enclosed in the cytoplasm, in which a vast number of chemical reactions take place, and which also contains other structures, called organelles. The prokaryotes, on the other hand, made up of bacteria, are constituted of isolated cells (this fact does not come in the way of their working in groups). Their chromosome, usually a single, circular one, occurs right inside the cytoplasm. It was as if, at the starting point of life, these two lineages, the eukaryotes and the prokaryotes, had branched off and produced the biodiversity that we now have. However, a study of genomes has revealed a third type of living being, as different from the other two as they are among themselves: the archaea (Woese and Fox 1977; Woese *et al.* 1990). We need not linger overly long over the label, which in fact reflects a persistent and incoherent obsession with the theory of evolution to find the archaic form of life. All of us, and all other living beings, evolved during the same period. The discovery of the archaea has led to a variety of interpretations.

While we do not know a great deal about the origin of life, we could say with a measure of certainty that there must have been at that point in time some mechanism in existence that gave rise to information of some sort. That mechanism has, however, left behind no trace, and researchers engaged in reconstructing the scene of several millions of years ago sometimes find themselves having to work with inadequate leads in their search. It is clear at the same time that there was a form at the point at which life began, a prototype of all living organisms of the present day. The uniqueness of the genetic code bears witness to the fact that being was baptized LUCA (an acronym for "Last Universal Common Ancestor"). LUCA certainly was not alone. Several other lineages must have coexisted with him, but they left no descendants, and today we know nothing about them. All these lineages had ancestors we know absolutely nothing about. Phylogeny starts from the moment the descendants of LUCA began to diverge. There we have a subject for a debate. One certainty is that the progeny of LUCA forms a three-pointed star.

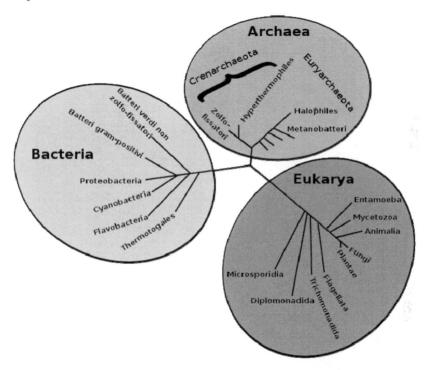

Figure 2.10. *The lineage of the three main living realms known so far*

We can imagine that the lineages initially split to give one lineage that produced the archaea, and the other lineage that produced the bacteria and the eukaryotes. We can also imagine that the eukaryotes first underwent differentiation, while the other branch produced the archaea and the bacteria, or that the bacteria separated from one branch that later gave us the archaea and the eukaryotes. We might believe that three options are the only ones possible. We would then have reckoned without the complexity of the evolutionary mechanisms and the brain of the researchers (and particularly that of Karen Nelson). There is, in fact, another hypothesis, which we can only imagine if we relax the restriction on finding a tree with a beautiful branch.

2.9. The tree and the web … and some complexities there!

An idea proposed by some authors is the following (Doolittle 2000; Theobald 2010). The descendants of LUCA gave us two branches to start with: bacteria and archaea. One day, members of the two branches came together, and produced the very first eukaryote. One provided the kernel, the other the cytoplasm, and their genes were then connected. This should explain why the genetic distances between archaea, eukaryotes and bacteria are of the same order of magnitude.

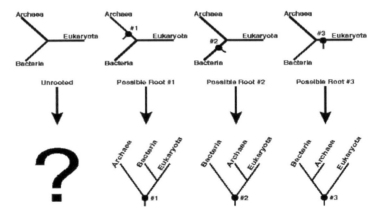

Figure 2.11. *As the three main realms of life are not rooted so far (left), several architectures of life phylogeny are possible (right), depending on the exact root location*

We know anyway that concoctions such as this appeared in the later period of evolution. As we said earlier, the eukaryotes consist of cells that have a kernel surrounded by a cytoplasm. Within the cytoplasm, there exist various organelles, two of which possess a remarkable property: they possess a chromosome, a threadlike strand of DNA that carries the genes in a linear order. This forms part of the mitochondria that are found in almost all eukaryotes, and particularly in all animals and all plants, and in chloroplasts in plants and algae. It was surmised that these organelles were in fact old bacteria "captured" or "integrated" into the cytoplasm of the cells. This hypothesis found confirmation through a study of their genomes. If we were to enter the genome sequence of the mitochondria in a phylogeny reconstruction program, we would see that this genome fits seamlessly into bacterial genomes (Mereschkowsky 1910; Margulis and Chapman 2009; retrieved August 2, 2016). It is the same with the different types of chloroplasts.

We also know that the sexual activity of bacteria and archaea, far less controlled than ours, allows them to capture one end of DNA and to integrate the information, no matter what the organism is where the DNA came from. We can then think of giving up the idea of representing the phylogeny of the living with a tree and instead represent it with a network (Mereschkowsky 1910).

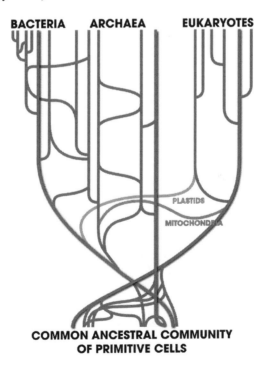

BACTERIA   ARCHAEA   EUKARYOTES

PLASTIDS

MITOCHONDRIA

COMMON ANCESTRAL COMMUNITY OF PRIMITIVE CELLS

Figure 2.12. *A more realistic tree of life (as a network) taking into account lateral transfers and endosymbiosis between the main realms of life (courtesy of Barth F. Smets Ph.D.)*

The reality is a little more complex and a good deal richer than one might think. One might wonder what it is that circulates along the outer edges of the network. Could one still speak of a phylum? What does evolutionary "filiation" mean? And is a phylum better defined by the information that flows through it than by the individuals that carry it? Should we redefine species and other taxonomic levels, and accept that the temporal concepts only find support in a perennial entity over generations, that is information?

The status of the concept of species has always been blurred. In the 1600s, when systematics (or taxonomy) was flourishing, a species was considered as a "type" created by a Creator to which individuals conformed – at the "whims of nature", as Carl von Linné thought. The nature of species was thought to be like that of the spirit. Linné and his contemporaries also introduced the idea of the constancy of the species across generations. Linné wrote that the Creator leaves to the organisms the possibility of "playing with their outer aspect, but never passing from one generation to another". By saying this, Linné denied the possibility of metamorphosis among species (*sensu* Ovid) while leaving room for metamorphosis within the species (caterpillar–butterfly, for example). This novel point of view gave rise to a revolution, as it were. If a species is not defined by resemblance but by descent, it assumes *ipso facto* a time dimension. Replacing resemblance by filiation has also been a constant element in the evolution of criteria of selection in taxonomy. There have been countless discussions on the status and the definition of the concept of species. We would have liked to define species by the individuals that compose it, its physical reading systems, and the length of its limited life, while giving it evolutionary continuity. But such continuity can only belong to information. If the concept of species is blurred, this is so only because we confuse two distinct elements that constitute a single notion: hardware carrying information and information per se.

2.10. When information and individual can no longer be confused

We may, under certain conditions, have to consider cases in which the existence of information cannot be mistaken to be a result of the success of the individual. This can happen especially if you are working in conditions in which different kinds of information clash because they do not have the same mode of transmission. One such case would arise when one is working with, for example, sexual systems in certain plants.

In the scrubland, we will come across an extraordinary species from the point of view of sex: thyme (*Thymus vulgaris* L). This species was first pointed out by Darwin in 1877 for the two types of characteristics it displays. Some plants produce large flowers, somewhat hairy, their stamens protruding, while others have small, trim flowers. These two types in fact correspond to the two sexes, not male and female, but hermaphrodite and female! Botanists have labeled the latter *sterile male*. The females produce seeds after they are pollinated by the pollen of the hermaphrodites (Gouyon *et al*. 1991; Manicacci *et al*. 1996).

The female flowers generally are smaller than the hermaphrodites. This phenomenon is also observed in some other species (beetroot, plantain, etc.). The proportion of females in many species differs from one population to another, but the species which has so far held the record is thyme. In fact, in the vicinity of Montpellier, France, the proportion of female or sterile male plants varies from 5% to 100% depending on the population[1].

Thyme is mainly pollinated by bees that possess the characteristic that they do not carry pollen over long distances. The bee, untiring worker that she is, only leaves one flower for another to look for nectar, if possible, on the same plant. When she has finished exploring one plant, she gets busy with another that is the nearest. She never frolics, but only works for the good of the hive. That is all we have to say on the subject for the moment.

The presence of these females, or sterile males, has long constituted a mystery. How could they have been in such large numbers that they seem handicapped (because they lack one sex) in comparison to the hermaphrodites? Now, as Darwin had shown, the females generally produce more seeds than the hermaphrodites. A partial explanation for this may lie in the fact that they, the females, reinvest in the female function the resources that had been saved from the male function. Going further, selfing brings results less good than cross-fertilization, and this will also explain why the females are better females than the hermaphrodites. However, this explanation gives rise to a problem: even if they were so much better than the hermaphrodites, their proportion in the population should not exceed 50%. In fact, in this case, the females would be the sole producers of seed, and the hermaphrodites the sole producers of pollen. The hermaphrodites

---

1 In populations comprising 100% females, the production of seed is almost nil, only occurring through occasional arrivals of pollen from a neighboring population.

would play the exclusive role of males, and we know that this leads to 50% males and 50% females.

Figure 2.13. *Flowers of thyme (up) and a bee pollinating and feeding on thyme flowers (bottom). For a color version of this figure, see www.iste.co.uk/gaucherel/information.zip*

The answer to this mystery must sound a bit surprising (Gouyon *et al.* 1991). While the genes of plants and animals occur in the kernel's chromosomes, some occur in the mitochondria, the old bacteria embedded in each cell, and play very important roles, such as in the function of respiration.

While some genes of the old bacteria disappear, and are replaced by the genes that had survived in the cell's kernel, some others still remain in a little chromosome within a mitochondrion. A point of particular relevance to our subject is the fact that, owing to their relatively small size, the mitochondrial chromosomes in animals carry fairly limited amounts of specific information. In contrast, with their larger capacity as conveyors of information, the mitochondrial chromosomes of plants allow their information to be copied and reproduced through descendants. In a large majority of plants, particularly in thyme, and, remarkably, in the case of the human being, the mitochondrial genes descend through the female or maternal route, and only through that route. Pollen does not perform that function in plants.

This fact has an unexpected consequence. Since natural selection promotes production of hermaphrodites as it works on the kernel's genes, those that are inherited from the two parents, it chooses the mitochondrial genes that cause the strongest possible seed production. From the point of view of nuclear genes, the act of producing a grain of pollen that fertilizes a flower also ensures reproduction through production of a seed by the female. From the point of view of a mitochondrial gene, what matters is just production of seeds. As a result, natural selection promotes the nuclear genes that produce plants making pollen and seeds (hermaphrodites), and the mitochondrial genes that produce plants yield the most seeds possible.

We speak of an evolutionary "conflict" between the genes of the kernel that constitute information inherited from the two parents according to the traditional Mendelian schema, and the mitochondrial genes that constitute information passed on by the female route. There are plenty of females when mitochondrial information wins, and plenty of hermaphrodites when nuclear information wins. In a majority of species, the more voluminous nuclear information (still the idea of quantification) wins, and the offspring are hermaphrodites. In the case of thyme, and other species in which there are females coexisting with hermaphrodites, the conflict is not resolved, and depending on who wins, there are plenty of females or plenty of hermaphrodites.

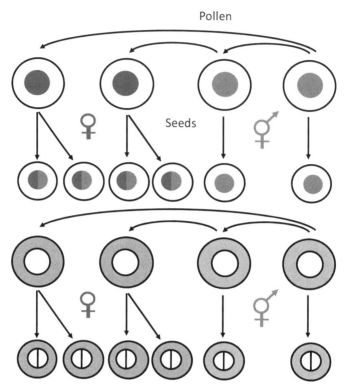

Figure 2.14. *A Mendelian inheritance (up) of plants, and a corrected conception of inheritance (bottom), according to observations made on thyme reproduction. For a color version of this figure, see www.iste.co.uk/gaucherel/information.zip*

The preceding narrative points to the futility of attributing an evolutionary success to individuals based on their sex. Consider a population of two females and two hermaphrodites, and suppose the females produce two seeds each while the hermaphrodites produce one each. Are the females better than the hermaphrodites in terms of natural selection? If we were to count the number of offspring, we would arrive at varying answers, depending on whether we took a nuclear-gene point of view, under which there was biparental transmission, or a cytoplasmic gene viewpoint, under which transmission took place through the mother. If we were to consider the genes of the kernel only, each hermaphrodite would have left on average twice as many offspring as a female, counting an offspring by a male equally as an offspring by a female. From the cytoplasmic point of view, the result would be different. Each female would leave twice as many offspring as a hermaphrodite, counting this time only offspring from the maternal route. We see here that it does not make sense to give selective values to individuals. We would have to give values depending on the mode of genetic propagation that we have adopted. In reality, there are at the same time nuclear genes and cytoplasmic genes that have an effect on the choice of the reproduction mode. One way to summarize this would be to say that selection promotes simultaneously cytoplasmic genes that produce females and nuclear genes that produce hermaphrodites.

It is the genes that are selected, and not the individuals. John Maynard Smith, one of the 20th Century's most influential evolutionary biologists, had added his voice to the growing support for this view. One of the authors of this book recalls an informal chat during which Maynard Smith said, obviously in a jocular vein, that if he were a cytoplasmic gene he would not produce pollen, and if he were a nuclear gene he would only produce pollen, for the simple reason that there were all those females to pollinate! Clearly, those refusing to budge from their stance of considering selection on the basis of individuals fail to notice the inadequacy of their approach in terms of the informational dimension. This inadequacy is found at different levels in biology, particularly in the ecosystemic context, and will be considered in Chapter 3.

The situation encountered in the example of thyme has been embedded in the framework of what is called "intragenomic conflicts" (Gardner and Úbeda 2017). These conflicts happen since some genomes have transmission characteristics that differ, and, because of this, the system gets pushed about in different directions. Many situations of this type have been found, and at different levels of integration.

2.11. Conflicts and levels of integration: avatars

In picking through the reading systems, selection acts on transmissible information, since it alone gets passed on in such a way as to either perpetuate itself or become extinct. Of course, the reading system, interacting with the environment and epigenetic information, reproduces genetic information, and thus has a key role in the process: it is on its efficiency that the future of genetic information rests, and, in a manner of speaking, becomes its avatar. The distinction between physical avatars of information and information per se makes the process clear.

Avatar	Information
Nucleotides	Sequence
DNA segment	Gene
Chromosome	Genes
Cellule	Genome
Organism	Structure of organs and microbiota
Population	Genic pool
Species	
Phylum	
Ecosystem	Structure of community

Table 2.1. *When possible, some correspondences may be identified between the disciplines explicitly involving information (right column) and those neglecting information (left column). For some of them, avatars and information types are reminded (central columns)*

This point of view has been somewhat obscured by debates about the levels of integration that selection was about. It needs to be said right away that, no matter the level of integration addressed, it is information that is selected through its physical avatars' capacity to reproduce and thus sustain it.

The levels we touched upon range from some nucleotides to entire phyla (the evolutionary lineages represented in the phylogeny). We know of phenomena that roll out on some nucleotide sequences in DNA. Small sequences, such as microsatellites, used in genetic fingerprints in forensic science, grow in the genome by using the replication properties of the enzymes. There are gene-sized structures, transposons, which have apparently no other function than to produce an enzyme that replicates them. At the level of cells, we can easily see that, in an organism such as ours, local selection promotes cells that reproduce themselves. Cancer could be viewed as an expression of selection at the cellular level. Individual interest and collective interest do not always coincide (as in society, so in biology). We know of cases in which selection for maximal reproduction of genes at individual scales can lead to the extinction of the species (loss of sex (Xu 2002; Hollister *et al.* 2015), for instance, or excessive growth in size). At all such scales, selection works through the avatar on information that is replicated to varying degrees.

2.12. Sociobiology, altruism and information

The different considerations explored so far were what had led biologists to recognize the importance of information. However, what is considered the hallmark of present-day thinking on information touches the evolution of social behavior in animals, including human beings. It is unfortunate that the approach set off ideological debates that have totally obscured the fundamentally innovative aspect of the information-centered view of evolution. The origin of altruism and, therefore, of sociality among animals assumes relevance here. Darwin had noted that natural selection appeared unable to explain sterile castes of workers and soldiers among social insects. How can selection lead to the production of individuals who give up their reproduction, and even their lives, for others?

A strong response has come from the work of William Hamilton who noted that a resolution of the problem might lie in the adoption of a point of view centered on genes and not on individuals. If we see a mother bird, for example, take risks to save her young, we understand that natural selection had prompted her behavior. The reproduction of the mother's genes has been passed on to the young. Why not to her sisters? In a majority of cases, there are as many genes in common between two sisters, or more generally between siblings (brothers and sisters), as between a parent and an offspring. From the perspective of the selection of genetic information, helping her sister would have been as "profitable" as helping her offspring. It would of course be a job to work out precise benefits of such an action. An altruistic deed entails a cost to the donor, or for reproduction present or future of their genes, what Hamilton calls C. An altruistic act brings to the genes of the recipient a benefit B in terms of reproduction. In reality, it is often difficult to determine the precise values of these variables, but we know that such values do exist. Given B and C, we can ask for what values natural selection promotes in an individual donor genes that strengthen the tendency to be altruistic, to help others. Hamilton's answer is remarkably simple. If we give the name r to the proportion of the donor's genes in the recipient (1/2 for a daughter or a sister, 1/4 for a half-sister, etc.), genes inducing a propensity to help will be better reproduced than those that do not induce such a propensity if rB is greater than C (Hamilton 1967, 2002). The value rB represents the net benefit in terms of reproduction of the donor's genes. It is this value that we need to compare to C.

If Hamilton's idea has carried conviction, it is clearly in part because of its logics as well as because it explains why we find so many well-structured societies among a particular class of insects, the order Hymenoptera (ants, wasps, bees, etc.). Determination of sex is peculiar among these insects: the males are haploid (they only possess a single set of unpaired chromosomes), because they are issues of an unfertilized ovule of their mother. One result is the fact that sisters (who are diploid, like us) have between them three-fourth of genes in common. In other words, from the point of view of genetic information, it is more profitable in insects to induce a helpful behavior toward the sisters than toward the offspring of these insects. This luminous explanation of an old problem has overcome numerous scientific problems. It was popularized by Richard Dawkins under the name "The Selfish Gene" (the title of the book in which he develops the idea; Dawkins 1976). It is child's play: behind the altruism of the nice bee that brings food to her reproductive sister, and kills herself working for her, there lies the intense selfishness of the gene that is only selected in order to maximize its own reproduction and that induces this devotion in its infinite selfishness. By helping her sister, the bee reproduces genes better than by reproducing offspring herself. Hamilton has noted that the effectiveness of a behavior in terms of gene reproduction should take account not only of the effect on the reproduction of the individual's own genes, but also that of the genes of its kin, weighted by the degree of relatedness. The "profitability" of the behavior in terms of reproduction of genes, in terms of the above nomenclature, is given by $rB - C$.

That this view of selection bearing on information was popularized with reference to behaviors raises a problem. It is just a step from animal behavior to human behavior, as biologist Edward O. Wilson cheerfully put it. In 1975, he proposed to treat human societies as he did those of ants, and to consider sociology as a branch of biology (Eberhard 1976). At the end of a century that had witnessed genetics applied to human beings giving birth to eugenics and even to Nazism, such a notion was so outrageous and unacceptable that many intellectuals and biologists rose up against it. In France, in particular, the idea of an influence of genes on human behaviors was considered a symptom of Nazi sympathy. In France, genes are (in political terms) right, while the environment is left. Remember that the poet Louis Aragon produced a 30-page tract to decry genetics and defend the Soviet pseudo-science of heredity promoted by Lysenko and Stalin. The summary proposal of Wilson's was rightly rejected. Unfortunately, the good idea, according to which it is genes, and not organisms, that are selected, was thrown out with the bathwater, all the more easily because of the times, when social scientists were relatively ignorant of biology. We still find sequels to this ideological choice, but its effects have begun to fade.

2.13. The "all genetics" versus epigenetics

All that has been said so far on selection acting on genetic information is in some ways irrefutable. As we have already seen, there remains the question of how epigenetics and the environment complicate the game. What is the autonomy of each compartment? Is there one among the three that has pre-eminence? A large number of geneticists are certainly convinced that genomic information is so much more massive, and so much more important, than the other two, namely epigenetics and the environment, that it has the greatest share in the determination of the organism's structure. The idea of "share" here refers to the contingent part of the information variation of a given context.

The respective shares of genetics and epigenetics in evolution, in the form which individuals have today, and the structure of the phylogenetic tree, or the network (see further on) of the Living remain largely unknown. What is strange about this point is that we may propose two schemas, both equally coherent: one in which epigenetics plays a primordial role, while in the other that role is near zero. On the one hand, we may think that genetic information produces nothing itself, that all that is produced is the fruit of the reading system, and, consequently, that the information contained in the reading system, in the organism, epigenetics dominates genetics. Conversely, knowing that all the molecules that produce the organism and reproduce information are synthesized from genetic information, and knowing that it alone has perpetuity, a capacity for replication and a capacity for the necessary encoding, we may think epigenetics is only a negligible subproduct of genetics. The two views persist, and it seems that more data are needed to settle the question. However, we can progress a little more with some reflection.

Imagine that we have designed a robot to which we have provided a formula that allows the robot to produce another robot identical to itself. Could we have made one form of life? We have seen that, from the perspective of geneticists, the robot could not have been alive because it did not originate from a process of reproduction with natural selection. But, in the following generations of robots, could there be an evolution that would contain life? To a biologist, it seems clear this will only be possible if the instructions to construct the "offspring" robot were not "hardwired" in the "parent" robot. Let us see why. Let us imagine that, for some reason, a robot is made slightly different from the preceding one, a "mutant" because of a slightly different part, or of an effect of the environment, or something wrong with the parent robot … This abnormal robot, from the fact of its anomaly, might itself produce abnormal robots. But, if the schema of construction were written into the structure of the robot itself, there would be a low chance that its offspring would possess the same anomaly as their parent. The difference would not be heritable. Therefore, selection cannot operate. Even a favorable anomaly does not pass on to the offspring since the individuals that carry it will not pass it on to their offspring. We sense here the limitation of the evolutionary power of epigenetic information. If, on the other hand, we were to give the robot a formula written in a language that it can copy into the next robot, then a mutation may perhaps be inherited, and evolution may have taken place.

A large part of an organism's information is written into its proteins, or "hardwired". This information is generally not heritable. It may play a role in evolution by modifying the selection processes in its genetic system, but is not subject to the selection process. Another part consists of chemical modifications of DNA (methylations), modifications that are copied during replication. Being heritable, they are perhaps subject to selection. But they can only qualify the expression of genetic information. The methylation phenomenon can have important effects, but probably cannot create anything new. The great superiority of genetic information lies in the fact that it is encoded in an elaborate language that allows a virtually unlimited scope for combinations. From this point of view, there are immense possibilities compared to those of epigenetics and the environment. It seems probable that there is much more information in the genome than in the reading system. Now, how is this point to be studied? We could start with the idea of quantifying information in all its forms.

2.14. What is Life?

In the 1980s, numerous works and articles by biologists and philosophers brought out the transitory aspect of organisms in contrast to the perennial nature of information. It became clear then that the revolution that Weismann had ushered in a century earlier had major implications in terms of the separation between information and its avatars: the physical entities that carry it, reproduce it, but do not *produce* it, at any rate, any longer. As we shall see later on, it has been necessary, right from the beginning, that information is produced by something other than itself. The physical entities, the avatars of information, are subjects of traditional study in biology. Organisms, molecules, cells and ecosystems are studied in physiology as well as in its reductionist derivations: biochemistry and cellular biology, and in its integrative version, functional ecology (that of biochemical cycles, elements such as nitrogen, oxygen, carbon dioxide, etc.).

With the advent of genetics, another biology saw the light of day, one that deals with information. This biology has fallen to the same level as its predecessor, but it does not deal with the same subject (see the diagram). At the scale of organisms, it has to do with genetics in the sense in which the field is commonly understood. It goes down to the level of molecules in molecular genetics, and at the integrative level in population genetics and in evolutionary ecology. The two ways of biology interact very little except in some molecular aspects. These considerations might be ground enough for one to view molecular biology as a fusion of biochemistry and genetics. One of the most obvious consequences of such a scientific dichotomy arises when one is dealing with the question of defining a living being by its metabolism. For physical biologists, who study the avatars, a living being is defined by its metabolism. We can see it as a coordinated assemblage of the flow of matter and energy. For information scientists, it is the reproduction of this information that defines the living being. They can then define a living being as the result of the reproduction of a piece of information under natural selection. Clearly, a mule (a sterile creature) is a living being (even though it cannot reproduce) owing to the fact that it is a product of the reproduction process. The two definitions are compatible, except at the two extremities of the level of organization and at biological scales. A virus is a living being to the geneticist – it is a result of reproduction. It is not one to the physiologist: it lacks a metabolism of its own and utilizes that of its host. At the other end, the Earth, taken as a whole, is a living being to the physiologist who calls it Gaia (Lovelock and Margulis 1974). It has a well-coordinated flow of matter and energy. This is not so for the geneticist. There are no little earths produced by Mother Earth, and no selection of those little earths that "worked" best. ... There has never been, at the scale of the Earth as a whole, selection of a quantum of information that produced an avatar adapted to its reproduction. The processes we have observed there can be improved by a selection of its parts, but not by a selection of the whole. We can see that behind some areas of agreement, the two views of the living world differ significantly, and some biologists and philosophers would like to see the concept of information disappear, so that they could stay in safety on the firm and hard ground of matter.

Physical Science	Avatar	Information	Information Science
Biochemistry	Nucleotides	Sequencing	Molecular Genetics
	DNA segment	Gene	
	Chromosome	Genes	
Cellular Physiology	Cell	Genome	Genetics
Physiology	Organism		
	Population	Gene Pool	Population Genetics
	Species		
	Phylum		
Functional Ecology	Ecosystem	Interaction network	Evolutionary Ecology

Table 2.2. *Correspondence between the various information types (right) found in life and its (material) avatars (left)*

Biology has discovered the part of information underlying certain aspects of its field of study: genetic information or epigenetics, signal transfer, so many expressions that translate this intellectual mutation. But if the word "information" is employed, what it covers remains pretty vague. The biologists are seized by the concept, though not its status, without working through its meaning. It is perhaps high time that the natural sciences took up this concept, tried to investigate it and, perhaps, quantify it. Else, those who want to discard it will be proved right. It will then become necessary to invent another thing to designate the same thing. Whether you call it information, structure (dissipative?), probability or rather improbability, there is something that passes through generations of living beings, through ecosystems and through human societies. This "something" deserves a more thorough analysis than has been accorded to it.

3

Ecosystem and Information

We analyzed in Chapter 1 the sort of information that is involved in human and animal communication. Chapter 2 showed how biological systems depend upon information for their survival. This chapter will explain how the concept of information opens up new avenues to improve our still-limited understanding of ecosystems. We will defend the idea that the ecosystem is a perennial system precisely because of its information flows and the encodings that sustain it.

3.1. An information-centered perspective of the ecosystem

The ecosystem is a difficult entity to understand for a simple reason: it is *invisible*. A forest landscape and an animal group, on the other hand, can be seen and photographed. When we see something, we are halfway to forming a mental picture of it. Some early 20th-Century scientists, such as Arthur Tansley, postulated the existence of invisible ecosystemic entities that did not resemble anything known (Tansley 1935). An ecosystem, in fact, is made up of living organisms (its biotic component) and inert things (its abiotic component). The assemblage of the biotic component, which forms the biocoenosis, remains in continuing interaction with the abiotic component, which forms the biotope. The ecosystem is thus defined as the totality of biotic and abiotic components, and the relationships that subsist between them. The relationships of importance in the ecosystem are all those that are needed for an understanding of its functioning and for anticipating changes that take place in it (Gaucherel 2014).

Thus defined, an ecosystem functions in such a way that the biocoenosis cannot exist without its biotope (even if it had the power to imagine such a thing), and that the biotope cannot exist (or, at any rate, exist in the manner it does) without its biocoenosis. A solitary bacterium in a Petri dish does not constitute an ecosystem. An ecosystem will only come into being if one includes with the Petri dish other aspects of the environment (the food, the local atmosphere, etc.). Putting these elements together does not suffice, however. An ecosystem is composed of several species that interact among themselves and with their environment. The interactions occur at large scale. The bacterium influences its nearby surroundings, by warming it, for example. One would consider it a biological system if the bacterium's influence were only local, such as that of an organism. If, however, the bacterium were to interact with the global environment from the Petri dish with other, distant bacteria, then one should consider the assemblage an ecosystem. This is why, for example, the human body is increasingly being thought of as an ecosystem with its numerous cells and bacteria that shelter in it.

Now, what is it that links together components that differ so much among themselves? Let us examine one of them: the biocoenosis that subsumes living populations belonging to the different species that the ecosystem shelters. Some among these species are producers, and they convert energy flowing into the ecosystem, solar energy, for example, into living matter. They are called autotrophs. It is with their help that plants are able to photosynthesize, and store in a biochemical form the energy they receive from the sun. The consumer species (called heterotrophs) benefit from the biochemical energy produced by the autotrophs. They include the herbivores and, indirectly, the carnivores. The fungi (which feed on dead organic matter), among them mushrooms, count as heterotrophs. They break down the detritus of individuals of the other species or individuals themselves at the end of their life. Ultimately, they mineralize the whole assemblage of the biocoenosis. Plants reuse this mineral matter, and there is thus created a cycle of matter that sustains the ecosystem.

One of the most notable properties of the biocoenosis is the matter-linked interaction, which we call trophic. The trophic interaction is based on nutrition and on a prey–predator relationship among species. The species of the ecosystem have other, non-trophic interactions as well, while all species occupy a place in the trophic network. We speak of a network, and not of a food chain (despite the linear view that we have just hinted at!), because one species may consume (or be consumed by) one or more of several others, for example, a fish that feeds on the larvae of its predator. The trophic network is a dominant feature of the ecosystem: it is always present, and its structure strongly conditions the functioning of the system. Imagine that we remove one particular species from the ecosystem. The resulting loss of trophic interactions will now affect the flow of matter into the new system in such a way that, by creating a new set of interactions, it may significantly change the functioning of the entire system. A classic illustration of this type of situation is to be found in the eradication of an invader species, such as a rat or a cat on an island, that would allow the ecosystem to return to its functioning as it was prior to the invasion.

A large number of interactions among species are non-trophic in nature, that is to say, not food related. There is an astonishing repertory of such relationships, some beneficial to the species and others harmful. The best known are symbiosis (two members of differing species need one another for their survival, as happens in the case of pollination between an insect pollinator and the pollinated plant), inhibition (also called amensalism, in which one population inhibits another) and facilitation (in which one population helps another to survive, without reciprocation). Non-trophic interactions combine with trophic interactions to build a larger network supporting the functioning of the ecosystem (Gaucherel *et al*. 2017). Finally, the assemblage of interactions among species occupies a place in an inert environment that feeds them with resources, and then collects the waste in a receptacle of abiotic interactions.

It would be tempting to see all these relationships as a string of pieces of information, transferred from one component to another of the ecosystem in a continuous to-and-fro movement. Such a stance would allow one to adopt a point of view standardized between the biotic flows and the abiotic flows of the ecosystem. Certainly, it is matter (and energy, as we shall see) that is exchanged between the constituents of the system, but it is *information* that helps characterize the structure of the exchanges (that is the topology of the interaction network). This is the point that we are going to discuss in this chapter and explain how an information-centered view of the ecosystem will complement the matter-based and energy-based views that are currently admitted in ecology.

3.2. Reservoirs of ecosystemic information

Where is one to find information in an ecosystem? Every structure that follows a non-random pattern potentially contains information, provided that its appearance was less predictable than it would have been for a structure produced by pure chance. Conversely, it is intuitive that the more complex the structure, the more information it can contain. The structure contains the information that we would need to construct it and make it work, if we could read it. The previous chapters began by detailing information contained and carried by our language, and then by living organisms. The distribution of the letters of the alphabet in a message is not random. We have already seen that the distribution of the paired bases of our DNA is not random either, even if the information they contain is different from that of language. In this section, we are going to explore the ecosystem in order to determine in what forms its information might be contained.

A particularly important constituent of an ecosystem is spatial information. This concept lies at the heart of landscape ecology, a subdiscipline of ecology that focuses on spatial relationships and interactions between patterns and processes. Richard Forman, Michel Godron, Monica Turner and Robert Gardner were the pioneers of landscape ecology and, as far back as the early 1980s, had recognized the crucial role of heterogeneity in the functioning of landscapes (Forman and Godron 1981; Turner and Gardner 1991).

Heterogeneity here is viewed as a structure, as the absence of homogeneity (that is uniform values of a variable). The observed heterogeneity is compared to the homogeneity corresponding to pure chance. Landscape ecology has shown how the heterogeneity of a landscape influences the flow of matter and the movement of organisms within it. This spatial information pertaining to the ecosystem is first abiotic, since the landscape is made up of abiotic components, then biotic too.

Ecologists later refined their analysis and their indices. Their derivations of the heterogeneity concept show improvements in accuracy and usefulness in interpreting ecological processes, notably those of connectivity and fragmentation. What is important for flows of matter or of organisms is not so much the heterogeneity in the support mechanism as the manner in which similar areas are connected to them, or the manner in which they are divided by the presence of areas of another nature (Gaucherel 2007). Quail in plots of wheat, or voles making burrows in the meadows, will see their populations favored in landscapes in which these activities are well represented, and with which contacts are more frequent. This observation is equally valid for species with very different behaviors, such as buzzards of the cereal-growing plains whose nests are distributed close to the distribution of land covers hosting their prey. Finally, specialists of the discipline recently obtained evidence in support of the belief that linear networks (hedgerows, roads, rivers, etc.) play a major role in preserving the numerous species and the biogeographical cycles of landscapes.

The spatial information linked to landscapes can be applied to ecosystems at much larger scales. The work of Jared Diamond, for example, drew attention to the importance of the shape of the continents (among other factors) in their colonization and in the development of human societies (Diamond 1997). Although these hypotheses are still being debated, there is no doubt that natural features such as mountain ranges, rivers, capes, or bays have fashioned our society, and thus what we are today.

When the spatial heterogeneity of a system is simple enough to describe, one may speak of its shape. The shape, which reveals a certain order within the system, finds its origin in the static or dynamic interactions among its constituents, in the forces to which the system is subject, and in the forces that affect it at its borders. The shapes range from the stripes of the zebra, formalized by Alan Turing, to sand dunes, from heat convection structures to herds of animals, and from leaves of a tree to gel faults. Note the wide diversity of these examples that involve both physical and biological phenomena, and include the somewhat rare combination of the two. We are speaking here of a combination in the ecosystemic sense of the term that implies equal weight (but not necessarily equal functioning) of the two components. Rarely do the physical and the biological marry as well as they do within an ecosystem.

So heterogeneity creates structure, and structure is the carrier of information. We might therefore say that heterogeneity stores information. Let us take the example of a vehicle, say a car, heading toward a destination. The position of each component of the car's structure is important for the working of the vehicle as a whole. The design of the car has located the controls (the pedals, the steering wheel, etc.) between the engine and the driver. One could, of course, cite counterexamples: sports cars sometimes have their engines at the back. These relative positions store bits of information which is not found elsewhere. We may not know for how long these elements retain the spatial information, but they do retain it. On the other hand, the information says that the components ought to be within reach, and in a certain order so as to be able to interact efficiently for a proper functioning of the unit. It is the same for all ecosystems: whatever the spatial arrangement of the components of the ecosystem and of their individual constituents, for a long time that arrangement stores a piece of information indispensable to the functioning of the complete system.

The spatial properties of an ecosystem are not the only ones that store a useful piece of information for its functioning. Arguably, biodiversity is also storage of information. As we shall see in the next section, a distribution of species rich in variety, which is not random, is often a guarantee of ecosystemic longevity. Ecosystems that one describes as rich in biodiversity are those that often show great heterogeneity in their populations, in their taxa, and in their flora and fauna (and also in their fungi and bacteria). The more mature the ecosystem, the more its richness, which is characterized by smaller but more numerous populations.

The information the biocoenosis stores is not the same as the information carried by the spatial structures of the ecosystem, even though the two types are closely linked. First, the biotope itself holds important information, which is not the same as the information in the biocoenosis. Then, even if one could imagine a non-spatial biocoenosis (in which space would play no role in its functioning, for example, in the case in which the individuals are all neighbors of each other), such a biocoenosis would nevertheless continue, for some time at least, to survive and to show a certain structure. If spatial information and information relative to the species differ, their significant correlation reduces the total information correspondingly. Species-related information contains part of spatial information and conversely. Species exist as they are observed, partly because they are spatially distributed. Conversely, the spatial distribution of the entire assemblage is explained in part by the presence of the species of the ecosystem.

Species could not exist if they were not in interaction. One could always imagine placing two species in a single enclosure, as they do in certain zoos with the herbivores, for example. But the animals would not survive if they were not part of a trophic network (or at least a trophic chain). This is what is being attempted with the artificial ecosystems that have been set up in confined enclosures (e.g. chemiostat and ecotrons) to study the responses of ecosystems to different perturbations. It seems easy to conclude that the trophic network itself carries certain amounts of information complementary to the foregoing. This is a crucial point because it will help one understand how an information-based approach might round out the approaches that are current in ecology at the present time.

Our car, heading to some unspecified destination, cannot function even with all its parts in place unless they are fitted in a proper order. Effective interaction has to be made possible among them, that is, there has to be a network of connections, of contacts between the gears and the driving belt, to ensure that matter and energy will flow to enable motion. The trophic network contains certain information that only partially overlaps the information of the composition in species and the spatial structures of the ecosystem. Similar reasoning would hold for the other networks of the ecosystem. The non-trophic networks, and even the interactions between the trophic and the non-trophic networks, also contain vital information found nowhere else.

We have just seen that the information carried by an ecosystem is stored in its spatial organization, in the individuals of its populations, in its trophic and non-trophic networks and so on. We must add two other types of information detailed in the two previous chapters: genetic information and communication information. An ecosystem cannot function without them. The biocoenosis is built on the genetic code, which stores a high quantity of information. The ecosystemic metagenome represents a different type of information to that of the assemblage of genomes taken individually, because of redundancies among genomes and because of the phylogeny of the species. The trophic network, the spatial encounters, the growth of genomes during epidemics or the exchange of DNA molecules and many other processes that are more or less correlated contribute to elaborating the complexity of the ecosystem's metagenome. The information associated with one part of these causes, notably the trophic and spatial relations, could perhaps be quantified explicitly, but many other causes of genetic complexity are still unknown to us and deserve to be characterized on the information plane. The network of molecular interactions, for example, is not reducible to genetic information.

The communication of information in the ecosystem is indispensable to its functioning. First, because many of its members communicate: the animals, and also the plants which sometimes exchange signals to warn of the arrival of parasites. The mechanism of communication, whether visual, auditory, olfactory, electromagnetic, chemical, mechanical or of another kind, influences the functioning of the ecosystem. Human language also exerts an influence, as Eva Jablonka and Marion Lamb remind us (Jablonka and Lamb 2005). The anthroposystems, the ecosystems modified for the human being, have a function much guided by human will. Our management of the ecosystems is still very rudimentary, but our footprint is to be found on all of the planet's ecosystems, if one is to believe the Millennium Ecosystem Assessment (MEA 2005). Even the ecosystems called natural, at great altitudes or at great depths, are touched by climate change in which humanity is the prime cause.

By analogy, a car cannot move without human information. It is this information that keeps the vehicle on the road, that turns the steering wheel, that works the pedals and that takes the car closer to its destination. Over the longer term, it is language and communication with a passenger or a geolocation system that guides the vehicle to its chosen point. The turns that it makes are chosen on the basis of certain criteria, and this leads us back to human information. This is not to imply that ecosystems pursue a goal such as the one in our car example to reach a particular destination: it is about imagining them at work, that is, heading to an unknown and undefined destination.

One form of information that makes a notable contribution to the functioning of an ecosystem is that which enters the system, and is contained in the inputs of matter and energy. Now it must be remembered that the ecosystem is an "open" system; each new input is an addition of information different from the sort of information that we have considered so far. New information results when, with variations in solar radiation, masses of air that are larger than those in the ecosystem under study draw a field of heterogeneous rain, or when geological time shapes rocks and soil in the ecosystem, and this new information will influence the functioning of the ecosystem over the course of time.

Information is stored everywhere in ecosystems, in all its aspects. Their spatial structure and their trophic structure also carry information that is not only long term, but also information that conditions the functioning of the parts of the system and thus represents many memory devices. Let us examine more closely the functioning of an ecosystem as it is understood today in order to discern what the concept of information is all about.

3.3. Biodiversity: an ecosystem made up of individuals

Can an ecosystem be summarized by the biodiversity that it hosts? Some people once believed it could, and some still think so. It has been asked whether biodiversity is even a useful concept for an understanding of the ecosystem. Biodiversity typically concerns the concept of the physically present species. However, this *a priori* position, under which species are artificially seen as the core of the ecosystem, seems unsatisfactory to us. A second meaning of the word has to do with the heterogeneity of the metagenome, that is, the aggregation of all the genetic material present in the organisms of the system. A third use of the term relates to functional diversity, which concerns interactions between species. We would like to extend the concept to all dynamical relationships that link the components of the ecosystem, and thus build an ecosystemic biodiversity. These definitions of biodiversity are internal to the ecosystem, and it may be possible to broaden the scale so that the definition could then include the diversity of ecosystems, a so-called interecosystemic biodiversity. In such contexts of intra- and inter-ecosystem biodiversities, where is information located?

Biodiversity is not just an inventory of the ecosystem's constituents, be they biotic or not. A first step in going beyond a limited interpretation of biodiversity would consist of considering the relative roles played by the species, rather than the species themselves. Species live together within the ecosystem. They are necessarily in competition, because they exploit limited resources. As George Hutchinson puts it, as a result of such competition, each species occupies a space *a priori* different from the space of the biological and physical variables of the ecosystem, a space that may or may not cover the space of the other species. The niche of a species is defined as the set of biological and physical conditions in which the population lives and thrives. There are many other threads of definition. Where and how the niches are located among the species will decide the structure of the biodiversity that we observe in the ecosystems.

Among the roles that species play among themselves within the ecosystem, demographic strategies are the primordial ones. Starting with the idea that species fight for their survival, Eugene P. Odum (in collaboration with brother Howard T. Odum) distinguished two typical demographic strategies (Odum and Odum 1971). Certain species assert themselves in their ecosystem with their sheer speed of multiplication (a strategy called *r*). They succeed with the help of different mechanisms, such as large populations, early sexual maturation or a large number of offspring during their lifetimes. These species generally have fluctuating densities, are opportunistic and pioneering, and generally lose out in competition with other species. They deplete their resources, and this often has a major effect on their host environment. The second strategy, called strategy K, concerns species that have successfully stabilized their biomass or their populations at a maximal value in the ecosystem. The species that try to protect their progeny possess low birth and death rates. They have the capacity to resist competition. They exhibit diversity in their niches, and are generally specialized, economical and not amenable to changes in their environment.

If species adopt such strategies, what about their communities and ecosystems? A result that Frederic Clements obtained in his debate with Arthur Tansley (Tansley 1935) was that the ecosystem usually receives r-type and K-type species, which are distributed differently according to their "maturity". Species responsible for the colonization of an ecosystem that has just suffered a major perturbation, for example, are of type r, because their demographic strategy allows them to settle in faster than others. Over time, species of type K create a place for themselves within the ecosystem, and bring with them diversified ecological niches. They multiply specific interactions and contribute to making their biotope more heterogeneous while reorganizing their trophic and non-trophic networks. Finally, the species stabilize biomass production. These observations were partly responsible for the birth of the generally accepted idea according to which an ecosystem's diversity gives it increased stability. The work of David Tilman and his collaborators has partly verified the validity of this notion, even though counterexamples have been observed (Tilman *et al.* 2006).

It must, however, be admitted at this point that links between the species' biodiversity and the ecosystem's functioning are not as clear as one might wish. The idea that two species could not coexist within the same niche was recently questioned by the neutralist theory of communities of Stephen Hubbell. According to this theory, certain (most) species are statistically equivalent at a large scale in space: they can coexist, having the same level of adaptation (fitness) and the same environmental adequacy (Hubbell 2001).

Alongside these measures of diversity centered on species and the relations among them, genetic biodiversity considers genes as basic building blocks. The current debates in the agriculture, food, chemical, pharmaceutical and/or cosmetic industries regard the metagenome as the first true matter produced by the ecosystem. The metagenome is constituted and distributed in time and space, and a description of ecosystems by their genetic biodiversity might play an important part in the elucidation of their functioning.

Some knowledge of interecosystemic biodiversity, which is related to the variability of ecosystems among themselves, may also help us to better understand ecosystems. Comparisons of ecosystems with one another gained popularity after the appearance of an article by Norman Myers and his colleagues listing the hotspots on the planet, zones in which biodiversity is maximal over a minimal surface (Myers *et al.* 2000). That marked the beginning of humanity's understanding of the diversity of the ecosystems that surround us, their richness and their fragility, their uniqueness (the endemism that characterizes the species one only finds in certain locations) and of actions to take for their conservation.

There cannot be any doubt that ongoing climate change will have serious effects on the health and quality of the ecosystems. The two main variables affecting ecological mechanisms are precipitations (water cycle) and the temperature, the effects of which are already being felt. A large number of species are disappearing, and new species taking their place, in the process setting off deep changes in the existing structure of trophic and non-trophic networks. Even the species that do survive in this scenario must change their behavior, with important ecosystemic consequences. At a broader scale, it becomes difficult to predict the future of the assemblage of ecosystems because any change in one affects the evolution of the others.

Numerous studies dwell particularly on changes in species distributions, such as the groundbreaking work of Camille Parmesan and her colleagues (Parmesan *et al.* 1999). They discovered, for example, that the areas of distribution of plants in the northern hemisphere shifted 6 km northwards every decade. Several numerical models are drawn upon to show, with estimated uncertainties, how a specific species will occupy the space according to predicted changes in climatic parameters. Thus, the species in an ecosystem will experience change in a way unlike that of its neighbors and will colonize new ecosystems. Ecosystems are in constant interaction, and ecosystemic biodiversity provides a measure of such interactions. Finally, it is the prediction of the sustainability of the ecosystems that is at the heart of this question: how will the movements of the species, and their gene flow, impact the fate of a particular ecosystem?

We have seen that the components of an ecosystem are in constant spatial interaction. An illustration: birds go to the trees that produce nourishing fruit. More interestingly, the colonization of these trees in neighboring zones depends mostly on the movement of the birds that they feed. Consider the jay that collects acorns for its own consumption. It is usual for it to bury the acorns (to avoid it being stolen) in places it may forget. A new oak will have germinated at each such place the next season, and then be pollinated by the wind. This dispersal mechanism at play is the main agent in the spread of vegetal species that, in the case of the oak, can exceed 500 m a year.

Spatial distributions still play a major role, and their importance in the ecosystem is well known. They are equally crucial between different ecosystems at coarser scales. Two remote ecosystems can, nevertheless, interact. The circulation of fluids that we have talked about (water, pollution, matter constituents, propagules, etc.) in the oceans or in the atmosphere creates a constant bridge between distant ecosystems and thus exerts an influence on their functioning. Obviously, these spatial relationships are not everything: it often happens, for example, that genetic adaptations and the plasticity of certain species exposed to climate change allow the species to survive in a place where one would have thought they had relocated or disappeared.

We have just seen that the biodiversity of an ecosystem does not shrink to the list of its species. We have also seen that several sorts of information pertaining to the species are embedded in the ecosystem: information about their demographic strategies, their habitats, their relative spatial distributions and their climate. We can identify the location of storage of information in every one of these components throughout the whole ecosystem. However, we first need to understand the species community before proposing a coherent view of this array of varieties of information. Indeed, we guess that apart from the biocoenosis and its populations, communities of species also contain ecosystemic information.

3.4. Phylogeny of communities: biology in the arena

The young discipline of phylogeny attempts to grasp the biocoenosis of the ecosystems through different markedly biological methods. The avowed object of the direction of the search is an understanding of the assemblage of the species, and ultimately their conservation within the ecosystems. We may content ourselves with examining the distributions of species and their characteristics in ecological niches. However, one particular approach that originated notably in the thinking of Cam Webb stressed the importance of the phylogeny of the species, or, in other words, their evolutionary history. His central hypothesis was that phylogenetically near species (or relatives, in evolutionary terms) must occupy ecological niches that are equally near (Webb *et al.* 2002). For example, mammals that returned to water (after their ancestors colonized land) are closely related. Let us now consider how a piece of biological information can contribute to the conservation of the ecosystems.

The phylogeny school believes that the distribution of the niches within a community results from the phylogenetics that link its constituent populations. Because of, in particular, molecular marker techniques and the associated statistical methods that have been in use for some years, the hypothesis has become more accessible. While this hypothesis is attractive, it should be treated with care. Nevertheless, using a combination of ecological approaches (features/niches) and biological approaches (genomes), we can get progressively closer to an understanding of the coexistence and diversity of the species in a community. We can perhaps soon make a connection among their spatial distributions, their networks of interactions and their workings.

Much of the promise of this phylogeny-oriented approach stems from the fact that it builds a bridge between biological information of the genetic kind and information that relates to species and their ecology. It also bridges coarse scales of evolutionary and regional types, and fine scales (such as local populations). To be more exact, however, the approach underlying phylogeny allows us to quantify collective genetic information into a higher organizational level, namely into that of species. Using these metrics, modified as necessary, we can quantify genetic information as it is distributed in a community through speciation (that is, the appearance of new species). We can also quantify the distribution of ecological information in a metagenome that results notably from its migration among different regions. Thus, the phylogeny of communities inherently studies the flow of information among an ecosystem's biological compartments at different scales of space and time.

This biology-inspired approach is at the border of the two types of information explored in this book, namely genetic information and species-related information. The information concept receives inadequate attention in ecology, as well as in biology, as we have seen. Can it now open a fruitful channel for a hoped-for synthesis of the existing analyses? The concept of information, originally theorized by physicists studying communication signals, induced in some early ecologists a belief that true progress in understanding ecosystems could come from physics. Such a belief was perhaps a mistake. So what are the most recent channels of research?

3.5. The ecosystem: a physical system or a biological system?

Depending on how it is viewed, the ecosystem may accommodate predominantly biological mechanisms or those that are essentially physical. We are going to show here that the two points of view can be reconciled with the help of information, a concept that is versatile enough to make a link between such implicity different processes. Such a reconciliation will benefit the ecosystem, a system neither exclusively living nor exclusively inert.

Biologists will be sensitive to both the trophic and non-trophic structures ecosystems are home to, to the spatial distribution of the biotic communities, and to their collective genotype. These properties are rather complex to study, and their dynamic articulation is yet to be studied in depth. The living component of the ecosystem is in fact a fully fledged biological system (Tilman *et al.* 2006). It follows the law of evolution, with gradual changes in the species it shelters over the long term. It has been shown since the time of Darwin that evolution is the result of random mutations of genomes under pressures of selection (which are often environmental pressures). We detailed in Chapter 2 how one piece of genetic information leading to organisms that are better adapted to their environment has better chances of being transmitted to later generations, and therefore of retention. It is the same for assemblages of ecosystems, all of which are constituted of genomes.

Some scientists prefer to adopt a purely physical view of the ecosystem. For them, the flora, the fauna, the soils, the atmosphere and even the human inhabitants of the ecosystem all can be understood in terms of physics, for example in terms of thermodynamics. Following this line of thinking, they limit themselves to considerations of matter and energy flow and balance (Odum and Odum 1971). In fact, the concepts of matter and energy are generic enough to cover both the biotic and abiotic components of the ecosystem, and the purely physical approach only helps to explain matter and energy changes in the short term.

However, as we have said before, the ecosystem is neither a system that is strictly physical nor a system that is strictly biological. It is, in fact, a hybrid system consisting of elements that require intertwining two descriptions, one with a basis in thermodynamics and the other in natural selection (Gaucherel 2014). We do not subscribe to the notion that certain studies uphold, clearly for the sake of simplicity, that the ecosystem can be reduced to its biotope or to its biocoenosis. The challenge before us is to elaborate a theory that will produce a synthesis of these complementary approaches. We see hardly any attempts toward that end, namely toward helping achieve a better understanding of this hybrid object, even though its nature goads us on. It might be a good idea to look at the ecosystem with one eye representing the biologist's vision, and the other representing the physicist's, so that we have a "3D" view of it.

To handle the hybrid and still-unfamiliar notion that is an ecosystem, let us compare the ecosystem to a car in motion, as we did earlier in this book. The analogy will help represent an invisible, little-known object (the ecosystem) in the likeness of a visible and familiar object (the car). Now, this car cannot arrive at its destination by itself. It needs a driver. For the car to make any progress on the road, the car-and-driver combination is clearly indispensable. Following convention, we hereafter propose to label this combination a "team".

This car-and-driver team calls to mind certain aspects of the ecosystem described earlier. All of the constituent parts of the car (plus the driver) are necessary if the car is to function properly. For purposes of illustration, we shall assume that the car's mechanical parts mimic the organs of a living organism (Figure 3.1). Their relative positions are important: for instance, the wheels cannot be placed where the engine is now located. However, a displacement of some parts will occasionally be permitted: the driver may choose to sit on the other side of the vehicle, provided, of course, that the controls are suitably relocated. Apart from their positions, the driver and the parts of the car's machinery have certain well-defined relationships that are important. The gearbox, located near the engine, can only function if the gears were connected to the crankshaft. The elemental interactions of the team that we have just seen could be taken to exemplify the bond that exists between the different components of the ecosystem, biological and physical.

Figure 3.1. *A car without its shell, and without its driver. Let's imagine the car-and-driver team in a similar way (from nouvelle207.free.fr). For a color version of this figure, see www.iste.co.uk/gaucherel/information.zip*

If we were now to turn our attention to the driver, we would see that they are made up of an assemblage of species that is essential for proper performance as a human being. Intestinal bacteria form part of the assemblage. The driver does not reduce to a genome, or a metagenome. We saw in Chapter 2 that genomes frequently cross over between species, and this behavior increasingly gives rise to their being viewed as synthetic entities, such as the communities or the biocoenosis of ecosystems. One needs to know that this metagenome also participates in the functioning of the team: it allows the driver to guide the vehicle. The human being, in this example, is at the end of the chain: they play a particular role. They choose the destination, never mind the fact that the vehicle is no less indispensable to the job.

The human being also has a place in the ecosystem, though a little apart. That place is present in both the biotic and abiotic components of the system, in the population and its activities that generally affect the ecosystems (Gaucherel 2007). We all know of indiscriminate deforestation, uncontrolled commercial fishing, excessive consumption of fossil fuels and wanton burning of vegetation, all of them obviously harmful acts going on around us that point to the need to take into account the anthropogenic component of the ecosystem. This component is also marked by the speed of change that it brings: think about climate change, biodiversity erosion, etc. The driving element in the team example, the human being, can communicate with a passenger or a geolocation system for help in ascertaining his route. An extraterrestrial being wishing to predict the team's direction on the basis of the team's functioning would also have to analyze the hidden human choice. The decision-making process involved (the interaction with a passenger or with a geolocation system), occurs through an exchange of information that is encoded in a human language. Likewise, we would need to understand the type of information the human being handles through their language if we are to understand adequately the anthropogenic component of the ecosystems.

Further, it is the entire network of interactions in the driving mechanism that we need to understand. Among ecologists, A. Tansley made this point quite a long time ago, but successors all too often equated that network to a network of species only, a network collectively labeled "biodiversity". These ecologists overlooked the inert elements in the chain that also contribute to interactions and the operation of the system as a whole.

We shall stretch this car-and-driver team analogy a little further to revisit ecosystemic biodiversity. There are many team units that populate our roads. The car park is an example of mechano-diversity, and it would be interesting to study it for its own sake. There is need for a regular supply of fuel and oil and water for the engine, and of food and water for the driver. The team is an open system continually receiving and/or consuming matter and energy. The combustion of petrol and air is a primary act of consumption that corresponds to photosynthesis. It feeds a generator that produces electricity which is then sent to other components of the mechanism (for example the radio and the windshield wipers), this energy corresponds to the biochemical energy in living elements. It would help to examine existing forms of teamwork in discerning their general structure and identifying the boundaries of their fields of operation, regardless of the contingencies. A vehicle may run on natural gas, or perhaps soon on hydrogen, without changing the basic organization of the ensemble. Similarly, ecosystems function most often on solar energy, but those that use the energy of the hot springs in oceanic "smokers" show interesting similarities.

Furthermore, ecosystems are constantly in interaction among themselves, not unlike the different teams we have taken as an analogy. Any movement of a team of the car park affects one or more of the others, as all teams are dependent on the road network, and none can easily leave it. This is a bit like the ecosystems that are dependent on the climate and the condition of the planet. When a countrywide restructuring of a road network is going on, local road networks and thus teams are also affected. In this case of ecosystemic interactions, the concepts of species and biodiversity become irrelevant, and it would be more fruitful to consider the ecosystem as an open reservoir of matter and energy. This is this complementary view to the biological one that the following section will analyze.

3.6. An ecosystem made up of matter and energy

The first global view that pioneer specialists such as Alfred Lotka had of the ecosystem was certainly that it was a cycle of matter (Lotka 1925). The regulating role of nutriments in different ecosystems was noted very early on. Phosphorus, for example, seems more limiting in freshwater systems, while nitrogen is more limiting in marine ecosystems. Nitrogen and phosphorus seem to be generated more rapidly by the litter of the tropical zones. Water and carbon cycles are well understood, and these cycles are now being discussed in depth in an effort to understand the roles and responses of ecosystems to the global changes now observed. One might still wonder today whether production in a particular ecosystem is limited by a fluctuating supply of nutrients (ascending regulation) or by the species' consumption of those nutrients (descending regulation). The two types of regulation probably combine in a variable proportion that is insufficiently understood (Frontier *et al.* 2008).

On a closer look, however, this view of an ecosystem through its cycle of matter does not appear satisfactory. We have known since the work of Eugene P. and Howard T. Odum that it is important to understand at the same time how energy is distributed in the system (Odum and Odum 1971). We often speak of the auxiliary power supply that ensures the exchange of matter that we have already described and which is indispensable for the functioning of the ecosystem. This energy is often of a physical origin. It allows circulation of fluids that carry nutrients and biochemical elements. Typical examples are the circulation of water within plants from evapotranspiration, and ascending currents in the oceans (upwelling) that bring with them the nutrients needed by organisms that live below the surface of the water. The energy needed for the growth of plants and the movement of living organisms is also a form of auxiliary energy.

The first analyses of energy transfers within the ecosystem highlighted the sizable losses of energy that take place from one trophic level to another during the process. According to Raymond Lindeman, only around 10% of energy passes from one level to a higher trophic level (Lindeman 1942). The rest is lost to the organisms at the bottom of the trophic chain, or even lost for all species in terms of calorimetric losses. This observation follows directly from the second law of thermodynamics, which teaches us that no energy conversion is ever 100% efficient, there are losses due to energy degradation or dissipation. The second law of thermodynamics states that the spontaneous evolution of a closed system (i.e. a system that does not receive either energy or matter as input) is accompanied by an increase in its entropy, in other words, an increase in its "disorder". The order may be increased in size (and, consequently, the entropy locally reduced) only at the price of having disorder, either of equal magnitude or higher, introduced otherwise. Clearly, any order that is locally imposed by the trophic system's constraints can only exist at the price of a little thermodynamic entropy at the level of the global system.

Still, even granting that these pioneering studies possessed validity, no ecosystem could be considered as an isolated and closed system, such as those sometimes encountered in physics. Even when the ecosystem has reached maturity (for example when its functioning and its structure have stabilized), it continues to change and to respond to its inputs, the energy and the species entering it. Of course, its dynamics might resemble a self-regulating state of equilibrium, a state called homeostasis. One cannot, however, ignore the permanent flows of energy, and also those of matter, that maintain the structure of the ecosystem. The system itself is dissipative, as has been shown by Paul Glansdorff and Ilya Prigogine: it makes the best use of the energy that it receives, and so remains far from the state of thermodynamic balance (a state it would have reached if the system were actually closed) (Glansdorff and Prigogine 1971). One may say that the flow of energy allows the emergence of more and more complex structures corresponding to a local reduction of entropy (the appearance of order, such as in the trophic network) (Gaucherel 2006). Despite this observation, the ecology of the past decades has admitted its inability to explain ecosystems with the help of thermodynamics alone.

To know whether an ecosystem is close to an equilibrium or only stable is a big challenge confronting ecologists. Stability has several definitions. It will suffice for our purposes to say (after Crawford Holling and his collaborators; Holling 1973) that an ecosystem is said to be stable if it can return to its previous state after a disturbance (such as an unusual perturbation). The stability of this state may be associated with the existence of an attractor. As we shall see below, a natural organization of certain ecosystems may not quite fit into such a clear-cut definition. While the variables describing a system are subject to certain constraints, as would be the case in an ecosystem, the state of the system across time does not move freely across all possible states (called the "phase space", and defined by the variables describing the system). Its trajectory may, for example, be closed to form a cycle, or even assume a characteristically chaotic aspect that may be called a "strange attractor" (although it has never been formally demonstrated for ecosystems). When a disturbance or a catastrophe occurs, the ecosystem responds, and its trajectory in the phase space undergoes a change in consequence. Generally, an ecosystem is considered stable if its trajectory returns to its previous attractor. This concept, which comes from the theory of dynamic systems, asserts that an ecosystem can be completely understood from a physics point of view.

This approach is often presented as being opposed to a more information-oriented viewpoint, but, as we shall see in the following sections, these two viewpoints are not necessarily mutually exclusive, particularly in the case of ecosystems and living systems. The following section details how the information concept developed in physics, in parallel with dynamical system studies, contributed to a physical view of ecosystems. However, this attempt to understand ecological objects, as interesting as it seemed, did not fully succeed.

3.7. Failure of the physical approach

Information theory, conceived by Claude Shannon in the context of problems in communication, quickly interested ecologists. Robert MacArthur, in particular, proposed quantifying the ecosystemic energy flows that Raymond. Lindeman had studied because of a measure directly inspired by information theory (MacArthur 1955). According to this theory, the quantity of information carried by an event is related to the probability of the occurrence of that event. It is intuitive that rare events carry more information than ordinary events, simply because they are not expected. Shannon's achievement lay in coming up with a way to quantify the information based on probability alone, regardless of the significance of the event. Using some key hypotheses, Shannon proved that the average quantity of information of a class of events is minimal when all the events are equally likely (Shannon and Weaver 1949). Many disciplines have made use of this theory.

Landscape ecologists, notably Richard Forman and Michel Godron, have quantified the diversity of land cover (agricultural and others) utilizing the Shannon index. The index is maximum when each parcel of land considered, whatever its location, has the same probability of being forest, crops or any other sort (Forman and Godron 1981). It thus measures disorder, diversity and local heterogeneity (Figure 3.2). The index is minimum when different types of vegetation on distinct areas are concerned. A cereal-growing plain, a closed hedgerow-populated area and an agroforestry landscape will not show the same land-cover characteristics, and will therefore have different Shannon indices.

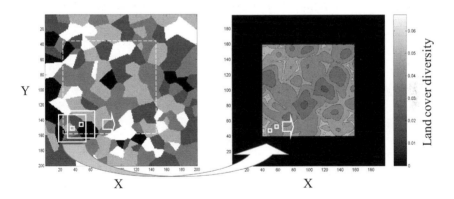

Figure 3.2. *Illustration of the use of the Shannon index to quantify the structures of a landscape. The landscape is a collection of patches made up of four land covers (various crops in shades of grey, left). The computed index provides a local estimate (in the white moving windows, left) of land-cover diversity, then projected onto a diversity map (right). The index values, in shades of grey, rise with the magnitude of local land-cover diversity, i.e. with the degree of heterogeneity in the landscape (Gaucherel 2007)*

Claude Shannon unintentionally drew an analogy between information and entropy calculated from physical systems, the two notions having the same formula. The entropy of the information, the known information content of a system, naturally holds data on the state of the system, the distribution of its constituents, similar to that of thermodynamic entropy. This analogy has been the source of numerous misinterpretations in ecology (and elsewhere), as we shall see with the use of extremal principles. It is in part at the origin of the negative perception of thermodynamics held by a majority of ecologists.

It is on the basis of this information entropy that MacArthur proposed to measure the state of a community of species in terms of the probability distribution of the flows of matter and energy in its associated trophic network. Despite this step forward in quantifying a community of species, the index suggested has been found to be incomplete and hard to measure. It does not take into account transfer efficiencies (the rates) between the trophic levels. This deficiency motivated Ramon Margalef to use the same index, but with its base in the present populations rather than on the flows at the base of their interactions (Margalef 1968). This approach has been reproduced several times, each time a little better than before. At the same time, one must take care not to overrepresent rare species that would, because of their rarity, carry more information in the Shannon sense than is expected. Paradoxically, it is easier to estimate the information content by concentrating on common species: rare events are difficult to measure.

The Shannon index and the products derived from it are in wide use today for a quick grasp of the structure of a community even when such indices have several traps to overcome. A first rule to observe in using them would be to interpret in a "relative" manner between the systems being studied: it does not make sense to say that the (information) entropy of a community equals 1.3; this would imply the existence of a reference community whose structure measures unity. It would be more meaningful to say the entropy of a particular community is 50% lower than that of a neighboring community. In this context, it means that the distribution of the species in the community is half as "diversified" than that in the neighboring community (that is that the distribution of individuals is more uneven in one community than in the other for a comparable number of species).

An index such as this can be valuable in quantifying the structure and possibly the dynamics of an ecosystem. In the case of the previously described maturation of an ecosystem, one would expect that an increase in the number of species (strategies r toward K), and a reduction in their populations, would have reduced their collective information entropy. One might even be able to quantify the contribution of each species to the total entropy, or the entropy between two species, or, in other words, to measure their degree of dependence. Thus, we have for the first time a metric for the information within an ecosystem.

These indices of diversity derived from information theory however present certain drawbacks. The first is an illusion of possible equivalence of information entropy (which measures the uncertainty in the system) and the diversity of the system. Now, the derived entropy indices differently quantify the same diversity. At the same time, a wide variety of ecosystemic structures may be characterized by the same information content. There is, therefore, no definitive correspondence between information and species biodiversity in an ecosystem. Another hurdle certainly relates to the dependence on the scale or organizational level at which the indices are calculated. The diversity of a community of insects is not at all the same if measured within a tree or over an entire forest. It is necessary to compare the values at the level of an identical organization. These indices pose many other sampling-related problems, so much so that it often becomes difficult to isolate an individual for the purpose of adding to or deducting from others in the species or community. We therefore sometimes calculate diversity indices on the basis of genera, orders or families of taxa within communities of an ecosystem.

More recently, we came across another important limitation of a diversity index built on the basis of probability, such as Shannon's index. Such an index has large statistical variability: it is sensitive to rare species, which are harder to sample, and the observation of which is subject to many hazards. A diversity index of this sort presupposes equal weight for the species and equal chance of being observed within the system, a supposition that seems a little excessive. Moreover, the index also presupposes that states (or events, or categories) of the system are independent. A hypothesis such as this would be illusory in a system as complex as an ecosystem. One would look for indices that take account of possible biases in estimation, such as the q-entropies of Alfréd Rényi. However, while frequently mentioned in literature, these indices are not much used in ecology (Lou Jost 2006).

We stressed at the beginning of this chapter the impossibility of reducing an ecosystem either to its biocoenosis or to the community of species that it is home to. These attempts to quantify species diversity can give a synthetic view of the community, but not of the ecosystem. Of course, a fixed community cannot exist in a similarly fixed environment, but this implicit integration must be made explicit if we wish to capture the functioning of the system. There seems to be nothing wrong if one were to wish to quantify the states of the ecosystem, instead of those of its biocoenosis alone. Given this, the first thing to consider would be a definition of the appropriate parameters that characterize the state of the ecosystem. If we consider an ecosystem as composed of flora, fauna, atmosphere, soil and human populations, then we must retain several descriptive parameters for each of these components (and their interactions), and then estimate the probability of the occurrence of their states in order to calculate the diversity of the assemblage.

So, let us explore how to quantify an ecosystem's complexity. The Shannon index and its derivatives possess another notorious weakness relating to a synthetic characterization of the complexity of an ecosystem. When applied to species distributions, this index is not sensitive to the order of the species, and we then say that it is invariant in permutations. The global Shannon index would keep the same value if the species of a community exchanged their respective probabilities. In the case of species, this could be a questionable advantage, if at first glance no species played a particular role. The invariance of a changed order has lower value if we base the Shannon index on land cover in a particular landscape, as some of its states may never attain certain probabilities. A network of hedges, for example, cannot fill the entire landscape, which would then no longer be hedges. Such invariance is also not at all suitable for application to a trophic network that is strongly oriented: the primary consumers and decomposers among the species higher up in the trophic hierarchy, whose members are necessarily restricted in number.

It would be instructive to work with an estimator that is sensitive to the shape of the probability distribution of the constituents of the system. This would be the case with the Fisher information. Fisher information, unlike the Shannon's index, can quantify the changes in probabilities that may be likened to a first approximation of the relative frequencies of their occurrence. In the study of a dynamic ecosystem, with a constant number of species, the probability of the presence of each species would, nevertheless, change over time. Returning to our car-and-driver analogy, a sudden rise in the number of intestinal bacteria in the driver (a result of a bad meal, for example) would lead to a changed behavior in the team, such as a halt along the route. An information index sensitive to the shape of the probability distribution of the constituents of the team would have identified this, and anticipated a change in the situation.

Of course, the index would have been too rough for one to guess with it in this case which functioning might appear, but it would have been a good start. In fact, the gains and losses of information that an index of the Fisher kind produces during such transitions are interesting to quantify, but they do not completely capture the idea of the complexity of the ecosystem. These indices remain very global, and convey very little information on the organization of the constituents. Fisher information, for instance, does not say if the sudden rise in certain probabilities comes from intestinal bacteria or from sand grains sticking to the tires of the vehicle (which would similarly change its behavior). A notion of organization or order is clearly missing in the types of index we have so far looked at. One remains confined to the spirit of the theory of information when one is working with the Fisher distribution. Instead, the algorithmic theory of information can be useful in quantifying the order underlying the organization and operation of the ecosystem and the team. We shall have occasion to return to this point.

No doubt influenced by the probabilistic attempts inspired by the different versions of information theory, some ecologists once thought that it was possible to use the well-known analogy between information and entropy to characterize ecological systems. Despite the aforementioned limitations of information theory, the notion of entropy still holds good potential for the ecological and biological systems. The extremal principles are among the several recent and therefore less established approaches that have tried to remedy these drawbacks. The pioneering approach on species with information theory was modified to take into account the interactions among different species. An examination of these interactions takes us back to the organization of the species community. Several indices that are initially informational, and later thermodynamic, have now emerged.

For example, the ascendency perspective proposed by Robert Ulanowicz relies on information shared among species, thus combining the correlations of the species among themselves (Ulanowicz 2001). The ascendency quantifies the independence of the populations in the presence of the others, for example, in terms of their respective populations. We might say that the ascendency is a measure of the uncertainty that one can observe in the network of relations among the species. This concept seems to be closely related to the maturity of an ecosystem that Eugene Odum defined, and led Ulanowicz to hypothesize that one community of populations tends naturally to enhance its ascendency, barring a disturbance. In other words, steadily increasing amounts of information are needed to construct a complex and mature community, because the relations among the species become more numerous and more diversified.

The increase in a pure information index brings to mind a principle the physicists know well: the principle of the maximization of thermodynamic entropy. The second law of thermodynamics asserts that during a transformation of energy within a closed system (i.e. a system not receiving either matter or energy as input), a part of the energy is lost in disorder, and therefore cannot be converted back into work. Such energy losses occur in the form of heat. This part of energy is quantified because of thermodynamic entropy, which can therefore only become maximal. We should remark that this principle does not preclude a local reduction in entropy, so long as the entropy of the whole system remains maximized. The maximal disorder or chaos corresponds to the thermodynamic equilibrium of the system.

Unfortunately, a direct transposition of these physical results is not possible in the case of open systems, unlike in the case of ecosystems, because they continually receive energy that sustains them far from thermodynamic equilibrium. We know from Paul Glansdorff and Ilya Prigogine that such systems react to this input of energy through a degradation and dissipation of energy that they receive (Glansdorff and Prigogine 1971). While the complex relations among the components of the system emerge, the structures that dissipate the energy present in the system tend to organize themselves. This point that has been mentioned in order to explain the organization of various living systems, however, remains a much-debated topic.

One might intuitively sense that an undisturbed ecosystem would tend to increase its organization, that is to reduce its entropy. Faced with the failings of a purely thermodynamic approach, several ecologists have tried to use energy indices of different types in an attempt to recover this intuition. These indices are state variables that characterize the ecosystem subject to an extremal principle to a kind of optimization (Gaucherel 2006). Among the best-known pioneering works in this category are those on the maximization of *exergy* by Eric Schneider and James Kay. Exergy is "usable energy" or work available for the system (Schneider and Kay 1994). The optimization principle states that ecosystems tend to use all the means they possess to create dissipative structures. These means contribute to degrading and breaking the energy variations (or gradients) intrinsic to the system that help dissipate the energy present. The maximization of the *emergy* of an ecosystem, that is the energy utilized by the organisms, is another track of optimization proposed by Howard Odum (brother of Eugene) (Odum and Odum 1971). Similarly, the principle of maximum entropy, which is occasionally seen to be useful, is less well established than the principle of maximization of "entropy production" in statistical physics with the work of Edwin Jaynes. In a general way, we ought to stress that these extremal principles are still being discussed and have failed to dethrone information entropy from its intuitive role in ecology.

To summarize, focusing on thermodynamic considerations, ecologists have developed principles of optimization hoping to quantify the dynamics of ecosystems. Their efforts have proved ineffective for at least two reasons: first, it is not certain that an ecological system can be characterized by a purely physical and thus thermodynamic approach, and second, physics has not succeeded up until now in correctly describing open systems outside of equilibrium such as ecosystems. Some wonder: would it be possible to achieve with statistical physics what a purely thermodynamic approach has failed to achieve? We shall see that there is a link between the description of the microscopic dynamics of a system (in our case, individuals, species, etc.) and the values of thermodynamic entities such as energy or entropy (in our case, those characterizing the ecosystem). If we succeed in expressing the dynamics of an ecosystem with the help of one of its constituents, we shall perhaps be in a position to come up with a global description, and, who knows, even perhaps to demonstrate the presence of a form of optimization.

What we need is not just the ability to measure information but equally, also to measure the organization of this information, the importance of which we have observed in the system functioning. This constraint is quite close to the spirit of algorithmic information theory, which is based on the notion of complexity (see Chapter 4). The idea is not to compare the structures themselves, but only to take account of the size of their most concise definition. According to this theory, most simple structures are homogeneous or periodic, while most complex structures are random. We shall see that the information content, in the algorithmic sense of the term, is linked to its complexity. However, measuring complexity generally remains difficult. It appears that such a measure is not yet able to quantify the complexity of the living. Other measures have been proposed, and we shall have to keep looking for a metric that we can use in practice to measure the information that ecosystems store, treat and exchange. There are other physical approaches emerging that attempt to enable an improved understanding of ecosystems, and some of them will form the subject of the following section.

3.8. Physics has not said its last word

When thermodynamics emerged as a science in the early 19th Century, with researchers such as Joseph Gay-Lussac and Nicolas Léonard Sadi Carnot, it was concerned with macroscopic variables such as the temperature, pressure and entropy of a system to which it is linked with the help of empirical laws. Ludwig Boltzmann and Willard Gibbs, around 50 years later, succeeded in establishing a formal link of a statistical nature between the thermodynamic magnitudes of a system and the parameters of its microscopic constituents. These developments helped place the concept of information on a formal footing, and opened a way to an informational interpretation of all physical systems.

We understand today the links between the three major classes of physical system descriptions: a gas, for example, is considered globally as a continuous medium, or a statistical collection of particles, or even an assemblage of individual molecules in interaction. In a macroscopic description (at the coarse scale), averaged dimensions, such as temperature and density determined by hydrodynamic and thermodynamic equations, describe the behavior of a gas. At the mesoscopic level (the level between the macroscopic and the microscopic), particles are regrouped in classes according to their speeds and their positions, and we study the changes in their statistical distributions, that is the set of their values. The microscopic approach (at the fine scale) considers gas as a complex system the elements of which are, in principle, discernible.

In physics, determining the conditions of descriptor transition from one level of modeling to another still remains a subject of research (Golse and Saint-Raymond 2004). The notion of macroscopic laws emerging through statistical aggregation from a finer level is a new idea that the ecologist community has embraced for its great potential. We have in recent times been looking to describe the set of the constituents of an ecosystem or a community through a statistical distribution in order to deduce their global behavior. The task, which is more mathematical than truly physical, is arduous. By manipulating the individuals and the species instead of particles and energy levels, those engaged in such attempts hope to discover the population distribution (abundance) in the observed species of different ecosystems.

Even though the analogy of the gas particles appears natural, it is hard to work with for at least three reasons: first, it presupposes a clear separation between the microscopic and the macroscopic states of the system (twenty or so orders of magnitude in physics, against the hardly three or four in ecology); second, as we saw with the application of the definition of Shannon, it presupposes independence of the constituents of the system (this might be evident for the particles, but is less so in the case of individuals linked with one another in a network of ecological interactions); and thirdly, in order to be able to explain the maximization of information entropy, or of average energy, or of the average number of individuals per species, there is need to define beforehand the relevant constraints that may have a bearing on them (Haegeman and Loreau 2008). Clearly, the transition from information entropy to thermodynamic entropy is not trivial.

The distribution of the population per species in a community is not the only aspect of the ecosystem that we may wish to explain. From a biogeochemical point of view, the distribution of the chemical elements in an ecosystem, for example, is a property that holds information about the flow and quantity of the matter present. We then speak of stoichiometric distributions. This category of distribution inevitably influences the trajectory of the system in course of time. The method of entropy maximization applied here calls for a search for the most probable trajectory of the ecosystem in the space defined by the concentrations of its chemical constituents. This probable trajectory is the one that corresponds to the largest number of ways of realizing the observed proportion of the constituents. As is the case with populations, the approach is purely combinatorial and therefore statistical, except for the constraints chosen in the maximization: conservation of mass and/or energy, for example. The system could therefore be considered either closed or not depending on the point of view adopted.

These attempts to understand biological and chemical components of ecosystems are purely physical in spirit. In a sense, they provide the physical view complementary to the biological view of the previously mentioned evolutionary attempts to understand ecosystems. At the same time, both the physical and biological approaches share the characteristic of being non-spatial. Space is implicit in them, and there is therefore no need to make explicit any relationship in terms of neighborhood or constraints on displacements among the constituents of the ecosystem. Ecologists have long known the primordial role of spatiality in the functioning of the ecosystem. The statistical physics approach that we evoked can be modified to take account of spatiality. A model that readily comes to mind is the model of Ernst Ising, which was developed for ferromagnetic systems, that is, materials that acquire magnetization (Ising 1925). This very simple but powerful model, first described in 1924, succeeded in describing the complex behavior of a material. Here, the constituents are atoms given spins, that is, magnetic moments that can point in two opposite directions. The distinguishing aspect of Ising's model is the fact that each atom influences the state of its neighbors by prompting their spin to agree with its own. The model predicts the probability of observing a certain spatial configuration for which the dominant spin will vary from one zone to another of the material. Under certain conditions, the emerging spatial configuration is much more simple and structured than we might expect if limited to a simply statistical approach.

This model was modified in the succeeding decades to simulate soap lather, cell tissues and such other materials. Researchers such as François Garner and James Glazier looked for parameters analogous to the spin in the state of gas trapped in the soap bubbles or in the state of the cells of a tissue in contact with one another. The constituents are then no longer atoms, but elements of another nature, such as bubbles or cells (Graner and Glazier 1992). The researchers considered states that could take several values (and not just a parameter "high" and a parameter "low" as for spin). They were able to characterize dynamic systems while modifying the distribution of these states. The latest cell models have even succeeded in explaining the cellular adhesion observed in certain tissues.

These approaches are based on the formalization of a function, the Hamiltonian, which summarizes the system. Now, we have known for a long time in physics that by minimizing this function we can configure the state of the most probable system. A recent study by one among us (Gaucherel 2011) has proposed writing the Hamiltonian of a forest ecosystem along the lines of these previous works in physics and biology. This very simple model, which is still phenomenological (non-mechanistic), accurately reproduces the distribution of the differences of the tree densities between pairwise plantations in a forest. A distribution such as this represents a spatial self-organization characteristic of this type of forest landscape.

Ising's model and its continuations describe cases of self-organization. First studied by Ilya Prigogine and Stuart Kauffman and their successors in the sciences of the living, self-organization corresponds to the spontaneous organization of a system under the effect of the interactions of its constituents (Kauffman 1969). This is the case when we observe the appearance (the emergence) of patterns or structures within a collective system formed of numerous elements of the same type. Self-organization is also at work at the moment of phase transitions in physics, for example when snowflakes of various shapes appear close to 0°C. Self-organization often manifests itself through the self-similarity (i.e. a structure that resembles its parts, as in fractal objects) of certain properties of the system. In the case of the density of trees, the self-similarity is to be found in the surfaces or the borders between distinct phases of the forests, the grasslands, etc. Self-similarity is an emerging property due to local influences (the presence of a tree often tends to favor the presence of a neighboring tree). However, self-similarity is neither necessary nor sufficient for self-organization. For example, the reaction–diffusion model, proposed by Alan Turing in 1952, explains the organization of regular spots and stripes that occur in the coats of certain animals without producing self-similarity. The approaches based on self-organization, however, remain today exploratory and far from constituting proved theories (Gell-Mann 1994).

There have been numerous attempts to interpret certain components of the ecosystem as resulting from self-organization. These attempts concern the distribution of the sizes of individuals from a community of species according to their metabolism, the distribution of the number of species on the geological time scale (biotic examples), and even the distribution of watershed surfaces in a basin (an abiotic example). More time will be needed for these approaches to be validated. We would not have been far from a general theory of ecosystems, given these recent attempts, but for the fact that they only pertain to certain components of the ecosystem. They rest on the biocoenosis or on the biotope, with evolutionary or energy considerations, but never the two together at the same time. The link between the two dominant conceptual frameworks of the ecosystem, the thermodynamic and the evolutionary, is still to be established. Section 3.9 divides this important question into more modest corollary questions to simplify the task.

3.9. The great challenges of ecology

The preceding presentations might create an impression that we know all there is to know about ecosystems. However, what we do have is an incomplete picture of the subject, and there remains a great deal to learn what ecosystems are, and how they function. A proof of this statement is to be found in our inability to manage them. We do know that the cyclic processes of transformation of matter and circulation of energy that we spoke of earlier largely determine the conditions in ecosystems. These processes contribute to what are called "ecological services": regulating greenhouse gas, production of drinking water or recycling of waste. They contribute to the system's functioning (Frontier *et al.* 2008). Now how are we to reconcile the many different and perhaps disparate elements of the system without trying to unify them into an integrated understanding? Just as information opens up avenues of holistic interpretation, we believe that information will also help in understanding ecological complexities.

An international report on ecosystemic services, named the Millennium Ecosystem Assessment (MEA), is something of a landmark. Released in 2003, it states that mankind has wrought more changes in ecosystems over the past 50 years than there had been at any time during the preceding tens of millions of years (MEA 2005). For this reason, we are probably experiencing the sixth great extinction-of-life crisis (after the fifth that had occurred 66 million years ago and had led to the extinction of the dinosaurs). During our time, erosion of the biodiversity of species has been occurring at rates exceeding 1000 to 10,000 times the "natural" rate. While contributing to improvements in the human condition, the changes we have brought about are increasing the degradation of ecosystemic services. This degradation will put at risk the advantages that future generations could have hoped to enjoy from these ecosystems. It will become harder to achieve poverty reduction and elimination of hunger and disease. Do we have a sustainable future in which we will manage our waste, and we will find food and energy from our environment? This is perhaps the greatest challenge related to the study of ecosystems.

In order to ensure a sustainable future, we first of all need to preserve the diversity of life. However, as we have said earlier, the functioning of the ecosystem is not tied uniquely to its diversity. Should we then consider a form of biodiversity more functional than those we have spoken of – genetic, specific and ecosystemic? Listing the processes and ecosystemic services, the method adopted by the MEA, however, fails to identify the rules underlying ecosystem functioning, partly because of the wide variety of the existing ecosystems. Species in a particular functional group, for example the photosynthetic species, might be sufficiently numerous and similar to show a predictable collective behavior. In contrast, it is difficult to predict the behavior of an entire ecosystem with a small number of species because the presence of a few dominant species can affect its key processes. Diversity seems to hold out some guaranty of security for the ecosystem, but this may not be so forever, and is certainly dependent on a variety of conditions. Understanding the part that biodiversity plays in the way ecosystems work is another major challenge related to the subject.

There is a third challenge to be taken into account, after those pertaining to sustainability and biodiversity: the impact of climate change on the ecosystems. It is a fine task to predict how the ecosystems will react (they are reacting already) to climatic changes. On the one hand, climate change has been seen to vary considerably over time and space. The rise of 0.8°C in Europe's temperature during the past century has been uneven in this respect. Some regions had more water than before, others less; some became warmer, others cooler. Similarly, ecosystems can react differently to a given form of disturbance, in this example climate change. Their capacity to respond is closely correlated to their spatial, trophic and genetic properties.

Now, even if we were to know precisely how each ecosystem is going to react to a particular form of climate change, we would still not know enough to predict the shape the biosphere as a whole might take. In particular, the ecosystems work according to a yet unknown coupling with the atmosphere. To mention just two examples, the earth's ecosystems exchange large quantities of carbon, dust and greenhouse gases that modify the atmospheric circulation on a large scale, and they modify the reflection of light on their surface (which we call the albedo) by changing dominant vegetal species that, in turn, affect the flow of energy on the earth's surface. Such global feedback are also met with in our team analogy: the car-and-driver teams that use the roads compel repairs to the road systems from time to time, and also compel the opening of new roads to reduce congestion, and consequently developing the national road network. In the long term, changes in this network are likely more predictable than ecological changes.

There is this one thing that car-and-driver teams and ecosystems have in common: their wish to survive. This is not about an intention to perpetuate themselves. Simply put, the very fact that they can be observed suggests that the ecosystems have survived, or in other words that they possess the means to successfully sustain themselves. The many studies that have been conducted since C.S. Holling and John Grime on the resilience and the patterns of response of the ecosystems show the propensity of the ecosystems to survive (Holling 1973). This is true also of their populations. It is in the interest of the vehicle and its driver to last until their chosen destination, and further, until the next one. Everything happens as if the ecosystem showed a sort of stability (or homeostasis) for the direct benefit of the life it sustains. The car-and-driver team looks to having its needs met, and to being kept adequately supplied; the driver would need to eat and rest well enough so that he can drive on to his destination; he may have to change a damaged tire; if several journeys are involved, he may have to replace parts, using those that have been manufactured out of recycled parts; when the driver has grown too old to do the job, he will be followed by a younger driver to carry on the work. Likewise, an ecosystem goes on by modifying itself without losing its identity. This is certainly the case with Gaia: it has to do with our planet, if we were to consider it a global ecosystem.

However, there is another problem here. If you were to ask an ecologist what our major misconceptions may be about ecosystems, they might overlook past challenges. They might reply: "The scales!". All the experts recognize the importance of scales, spatial and temporal, in the multiscale functioning of ecosystems. All recognize also that we do not yet possess the means to elucidate their role in ecological mechanisms. The term "multiscale" is ambiguous: it covers scales as well as the levels of organization. Now, the levels of organization are discrete, while scales correspond to quantitative and continuous gradations. The processes operating at a specific level of organization (the cell, the individual, the population, the ecosystem, etc.) are not the same as those at other levels. Conversely, a given process may be found to exist at two different levels. This property is called "scale invariance". For example, atmospheric turbulences that transfer energy among convection cells of increasing sizes may be observed at the scale of a simple current of air up to the scale of a country.

Another example of scale invariance is seen in fractal objects, a notion that we owe to Benoit Mandelbrot. These objects are the results of a recursive pattern, which means that the pattern repeats itself at every scale, a property known as self-similarity (Mandelbrot 1983). When one is looking at a snow crystal, it is usually not possible to know at what particular scale the viewing is taking place: each crystal has a seemingly endless series of scales in it. The characteristic of an object that appears similar at different scales carries information on the structure of that object. Does it tell us anything about the operation that created the object? Yes, it does, in cases of certain physical systems (avalanches, hydrographic networks, etc.) or biological systems (lungs, trees, etc.). But, in general, it is often very difficult to go back to the processes at the origin of the observed scale invariance.

In the living being, and *a fortiori* within the ecosystem, it is rare to observe these laws of scale at work in more than two or three orders of magnitude. The reason for this is simple: except in the case of well-known types of biota (plankton, some kinds of vegetation), it is rare to see the same pattern across scales because of the presence of many levels of organization associated with them. These levels of organization, which differ considerably in nature and function, are associated with dissimilar processes that have their own scales, and these are incompatible with scale invariance. The early attempts to understand the role of the scales in ecology had been to study the interactions of a pair of consecutive levels. The "metapopulation theory", for example, is about a collection of individuals distributed over several habitats, and seen as a population of populations. Simon Levin pioneered studies in that field of ecology by singling out demographic processes that occur in each habitat (growth and death of a population) and the migrations that link the local populations of these habitats among them (the setting up of a new population becomes possible with contributions from other populations) (Levin 2007). From this two-scale system arises the fact that a metapopulation in which each population is growing, but possibly destroyed by a disturbance, may be on the point of extinction if the rate of colonization in new places is lower than the rate of extinction of the local populations.

When the number of levels is large, there naturally appears some sort of hierarchy between the finest and the coarsest among them. This theory, proposed by Allen and Star, allows a separation of ecological processes according to their own levels, and an insight into their temporal and spatial interconnections (Allen and Starr 1982). The growth of a tree, which can be placed on a fine spatial scale, herbivorous feeding, widely spread, and fires, that can extend far, are ecological processes that each possess their own dominant scale. It is an intuitive fact that processes at fine levels (short distances and short durations) are often the initial conditions for processes involved at coarser levels, which in turn often act as constraints for them.

The ecosystem is a complex system, in that the concept embraces several levels of organization at the same time. We believe that this multiplicity of scales is in large part responsible for our difficulty in understanding the ecosystem. The ecosystem is the heart of so-called emergent phenomena, that is, of those phenomena that were not expected from their component interactions at the lower levels of the organization. This observation on emergence might also be made for several successive levels. It is therefore necessary for us to understand and codify all levels if we are to understand the functioning and the organization of the ecosystem.

We would not have completed our overview of our ignorance of ecology until we have cited recent attempts to discover the role of evolution (in the sense of natural selection) in ecosystems. It would be easy to show that ecosystems change and that the processes they go through are dynamic. We also know that the biocoenosis of an ecosystem evolves through a change over the long term in species in it as a result of natural selection. Now, does the ecosystem itself evolve? Note here that the word "evolution" is to be understood in a sense different from that of biology, given that an ecosystem differs fundamentally from an assemblage of genes, individuals, and species. The ecosystem contains abiotic components that give it a long-term dynamic that is different from that of a biological organism. But how is it different? This question continues to pose a challenge to ecologists.

Let us return to the notion of evolution in order to examine whether an ecosystem evolves or not. In population genetics, four principal forces are conventionally considered the engine of the evolution of life. These forces act positively or negatively on biological diversification. This concerns mutation, migration or dispersal of species within habitats, selection, and genetic drift. To this list must be added epigenetic and cultural processes. For a good understanding of the diversity of ecosystems through an evolutionary approach, we must first check if this diversity is stable, if it is inheritable, if it is of a genetic origin, and if it is selected. We then should examine if the mechanism underlying the diversity contributes to an understanding of ecosystems. We already know that genetics is not the only factor responsible for the observed phenomena.

No ecosystem reproduces itself, or, to put it another way, no ecosystem produces copies of itself, or undergoes a kind of mutation of its characteristics. No ecosystem appears to be selected on the basis of such a mutation. Contrarily, the ecosystem has changes of state. One could imagine that successive states might prove to be more or less favorable to their survival and sustainability. Now, the ecosystem has a partly genetic character, and, clearly, succeeding states inherit some characteristics. These states are preserved and stabilized, as is shown by frequently observed homeostatic situations. On can hypothesize that the complex interactions within an ecosystem sometimes produce heritable changes in the ecosystem as a whole. This could be the case, for example, with the productivity of the biomass (the mass of the living component) of an ecosystem made up of hundreds of species. These collective parameters depend on abiotic components as much as on biotic components, and we wonder whether they may appear to be heritable by the entire ecosystem subjected to the pressures of selection.

Such experiments are actively tried and would accord well with the idea some biologists have of evolution. They believe, as some among us have explained, that evolution works at all levels of organization (molecules, individuals, groups, etc.) simultaneously (Gliddon and Gouyon 1989). At the same time, one selection at a lower level seems to often dominate all the higher levels. This hypothesis, however, is yet to be confirmed. It is too early to definitively ratify the evolutionary experiments carried out on the ecosystems, but they possess the merit that they approach a crucial question relating to an understanding of these systems.

Let us change the scale. The planet Earth constitutes an ecosystem. This planet shelters living organisms and inert components in continuous interaction. It regularly receives energy and matter from its environment, the solar system. It is a system in non-equilibrium situated far from the thermodynamic equilibrium that it would have attained if it were a closed system. Physicists are familiar with this phenomenon. The work of Stuart Kauffman and Per Bak in particular tells us that such systems, open and outside equilibrium, can sometimes organize themselves. These systems possess an organization (in the sense of increasing order) that is the result of a global optimization of the system. This optimization can direct energy flows, as is often seen on the surface of the earth. Today, there is growing evidence in support of the idea that natural selection has close similarity to the concept of optimization that is apparent in other self-organizing systems (Solé and Bascompte 2006). The principle of natural selection implies maximization of the selective value (adaptation to the environment and success in reproduction). Some authors do not hesitate to advance the view that natural selection is optimization similar in nature to the optimization of the physical systems, which enhances the efficiency of energy dissipation.

What is one to deduce for ecosystems that are neither completely physical nor completely biological? If it is a fact that they usually dissipate their energy inputs, do they optimize their organization in order to do so? Motor racing affords a simple analogy that will help us answer these questions. Now, how does the driving team attempt to arrive first at the designated destination? First of all, it intends to reach the destination. Then come improvements to the engineering of the vehicle to arrive first: the choice of the vehicle, the condition of the vehicle, the condition of the route, the physical condition of the driver and the skill of the driver are all important. Finally, all other things being equal, there still remains the need to optimize the paths and to minimize loss of time by a proper handling of the available energy (appropriate accelerating and braking operations and adequate fuel).

An interesting variation of the race, closer than one could imagine in nature, would involve arriving at the destination within a specified time span, but with the least possible use of energy. The crew might act in concert with other crews or alone on a circuit closed for the event as is done for rallies. Only if it wins the race can the crew leave, and must work as a team over a longer term in a competitive season. Growing numbers of ecologists believe that ecosystems similarly optimize themselves in order to ensure their sustainability. Support for this belief comes from the homeostasis and self-organization that we have already mentioned. Another related concept is that of resilience, a property that helps the ecosystem to return to its previous state after a disturbance.

A unified view of ecosystems might help tackle the questions that we have glimpsed so far. However, while it has a bearing on the evolution of the ecosystem, on its response to climate change, on the role of biodiversity in its functioning, and on planning for its better management, no universal rule by itself today applies to all ecosystems. Today, a theoretical corpus is lacking that is capable of bringing about a synthesis between the physical approaches and the biological approaches, between thermodynamics and the evolution of ecosystems. The preceding sections have shown the ways biodiversity and information concepts first seemed to provide a solution. The following sections propose improvements of the informational view for ecology.

3.10. Flow and balance of ecosystemic information

How can the concept of information help us in our quest for ecosystemic unity? Let us go back to the beginning of this chapter, and try first of all to understand how, if a piece of information has been effectively stored in an ecosystem, it was formed and from where it came. It is by identifying the process linked to the information of an ecosystem that we shall gradually succeed in delineating its role in the way the ecosystem works.

It is not easy to explain how information can be created "beginning with nothing/from scratch". Astrophysicists imagined an inflationary phase of the universe to explain the birth of the stars from the heterogeneities of the primordial soup. Biologists, among them Stanley Miller, posit a combination of compounds and an energy input to explain the appearance of life. We guess that it is not enough to merely deploy matter and energy to make the system work, particularly if it possesses a biotic component. In the case of the car-and-driver team, it is not enough to press the pedals to move it (an energy-dependent action): the action must be performed at the right moment. What is presupposed is an important piece of information about the operation of the vehicle, the constraints from the road network and the rules to follow with regard to nearby vehicles. All this is external to the vehicle, corresponding to information acquired elsewhere, during the learning by the driver, during their driving lessons and from their memory of the local road network. Even though not material in nature, this body of information becomes an internal part of the system the moment the driver gets into his seat and starts up the engine. There has been a flow of information from outside the ecosystem (assuming definable limitations to the system) toward its interior.

Since any information entering can modify the material organization of a system, we may say that information creates information, overlooking for the moment the need for it to have a material support. We return to an idea that we have already touched upon, namely that a piece of information is capable of producing action: remember your act of turning the first page of this book? It is a philosophical question to determine if we could return to the set of material interactions, which had led to the writing of the message which in turn led the reader to turn the page. But it is possible and useful to synthesize the causes in a piece of information which emerged from the mind of the author and moved to the mind of the reader, after having passed over the page of this book. If the driver of the vehicle had available to him a unique stroke of the pedal with which to drive the team, he would have used the same amount of initial energy, the same matter inputs, the same genetic materials and the same network of connections among the team's constituents disposed according to the same spatial distribution, regardless of when he might decide to do so. The statement that the choice of the use of the pedal is informational in nature is seen to exemplify an extraordinary economy of description. It is the same as when we describe the operation of a computer at a given moment in terms of a program, and therefore of the information given by the programmer, rather than in terms of electrons and spins.

According to the description that we have adopted, the flow of information takes place within the ecosystem and within its environment. These flows occur everywhere and help link the components of the ecosystem with one another, to help keep the assemblage in action. The example of a national park may illustrate this statement: the park possesses a relief and heterogeneous soils (therefore charged with information), from the fact of its geological history; it receives heterogeneous precipitations in the rainy season; due to runoffs the soil collects the water in a heterogeneous way, but differently from that of the precipitations; the vegetation adjusts itself in part to this heterogeneity, which then influences the higher trophic levels; the herbivores and then the carnivores are distributed in a heterogeneous way in the park, and they in turn have an effect on the vegetation that is subject to the animal pressure affecting its distribution and its modified heterogeneity; this directs the park's waters, modifies the spatial pattern of the evapotranspiration (the process by which water is released by the vegetation) and affects in turn the cells of convection (atmospheric movements) overhanging the park.

The information chain that gave rise to the structures of the ecosystem that could be observed might have unrolled with the same flows of matter and energy, but producing another result. An information-orientated description based on thermodynamics would suggest that the observed sequence might have been produced because it was the one that had the greatest number of ways it could be realized, i.e. it was the most probable outcome. At a larger scale of time and space, similar spatial mechanisms would be produced: let us remember allopatric speciation, in which geographic separation leads two subpopulations to genetically diverge. The species retain the footprint of the heterogeneity of the milieu, its rivers and its mountains that constitute barriers to the flows of genes. All the biogeographical studies testify to this information flow, from one component of the ecosystem to another, in the previous example, that of spatial information toward genetic information. Flows of information, therefore, play a primordial role in the construction of any ecosystem.

Finally, when you think flows, you think dynamics. The transfer of information from one place of storage to another takes a certain duration. Oceanic and atmospheric fluids may react quickly enough to a change in insolation (the energy of sunlight). The earth's crust and its relief are slower to submit to assaults from the climate (erosion) or from human beings. There is a historic dimension to some flows of information whether for the biotope (geology) or the biocoenosis (evolution). The flows of information leading to the press of the car's pedal to take a certain course presuppose a piece of information patiently acquired during driving lessons or while learning the local road network.

Although we may sense the importance of the most recent approaches using statistical physics that we have mentioned, the efforts actually exerted to quantify the information and the flow of information have been limited. This raises other questions and demands for new methodologies: how to quantify information with such a generality, and with what index? What information? How can we define ecosystemic components that accommodate the flows? The problems are numerous, and we are going to examine some of them. With information at our disposal, it is fascinating to deal with a concept generic enough to allow a description of the exchanges among components of very different nature, between the biotope and the biota, and between carrots and clouds.

We propose here an information-based analysis of ecosystems. Let us imagine that we have succeeded in quantifying the flow of information and its dynamics among the floral and faunal components of an ecosystem. It is probable that by itself alone this flow may not be particularly informative. As we have already said earlier in regards to spatial analyses, it is only in relative terms that we can interpret the concept of information. We would like to know if this flow of information is higher than that observed among the same components of the neighboring ecosystem. If that were the case, we would have clues on the operation of the faunal–floral interaction in general: a higher flow would mean a more complex interaction, of which the structure in time and space is less random or less trivial (not proportional) and less stationary (more variable), perhaps. We would have been slightly closer to understanding the ecosystem.

Such understanding requires a comparison of information flows, not just among the same components of different ecosystems (as might be the case with an analysis of a specific process of an ecosystem), but among different components of the same ecosystem (Gaucherel *et al.* 2017). What are the interactions among components that dominate within the ecosystem functioning? The question might appear superficial: all components play roles, probably in equal measure. Recall the discussion on the respective roles of the motorbike and the rider in achieving victory (Chapter 2). When the modelers simulate on their computer the biomes (the vegetal cover types) of the continents, they take account of a multitude of factors of biotic and abiotic nature: the soils, the climate, the fires, etc. They give these factors relative importance in a more or less empirical way with their equations, but the relative importance in the final result remains variable. The modelers empirically know, for example, that at the large scale the climate has much greater weight than do the other factors. They often modify the "fire factor" because fires, natural or not, are little known in order to adjust the model to their observations.

Whether or not the parts accorded to the different flows of information are equal, it is important to quantify them in order to have a view of the total body of information that the ecosystem receives and contains. For this reason, we are proposing that an information balance is at work for the ecosystems. Several balance sheets have already been developed in ecology, certainly those on matter and on energy, or those linked to the natural elements (e.g. carbon and nitrogen cycles). These flows transfer information, but are still matter. We are suggesting the adoption of an additional form of balance sheet of information. This information balance, complementary to the others, has not yet been studied, and it will probably teach us more about the functioning of the whole system.

The information balance sheet may be null, positive or negative, but at the heart of the matter there is the question of how to differentiate stored information from information that has been exchanged, biotic information from abiotic information, or created information from received information. It is useful to rank these quantities of information in order to understand their cycle within the ecosystem. An extraterrestrial trying to understand how the car-and-driver team succeeds in reaching its destination would need to differentiate the pieces of information according to which the car or the driver they came from. The alien will no doubt detect a store of lower-level energy in the driver compared with that of the vehicle, but it would surely identify the flow of information from the first to the second (press the pedal, turn the steering wheel, etc.), and its correlation with the road network. With the information balance sheet, we may hope that the observer understands the importance of the information acquired in other respects (the driving rules) and transferred to the operation (the driving itself). Will the identification of these flows and their balance sheet suffer? Probably not, and without a clear view of the rules that govern these flows, we would only have covered part of the way.

3.11. Ecosystemic codes

The ecosystem is an immense reservoir of information and is at the same time the place of numerous information flows. In what manner could this assessment help us understand the working of an ecosystem? One way might be in predicting the direction in which the ecosystem is going to change. An ecosystem possesses a metagenome, certain parts of which evolve, in interaction with its own environment, and which itself undergoes change. How may we make a link between the information that an ecosystem carries and the information that is linked to its changes? Is it possible that, if it evolves in a certain way, as in optimization, for example, the information content of the ecosystem keeps track of it, and probably even contributes to its evolution? This implies a question about the future of the information at a large scale in time and space. Beyond the identification of the information and its flows within the ecosystem, we defend the idea that codes are associated with this information and its transport/exchange. Let us study them.

The information that helped us understand the working in the short term of the car-and-driver team moving toward its destination can also be part of a broader body of information that "justifies" the presence of the other teams at work. With a broader view, it might even justify past and future teams: it can explain the possible destinations by the spatial distributions of the drivers, by their current lifestyle, by society and/or by the economy that guides the production of the vehicles of such teams. To be able to do this, we must have knowledge of how the information is stored, and how it is exchanged.

Auditory (acoustic) information cannot be stored in its original form longer than it takes to hear it. In contrast, a bird can react to it by an action (evading a predator, building a nest) that will perhaps be long lasting. Together, these pieces of information can have an effect at a larger scale, such as on the survival of a population. There is a hierarchy among pieces of information partly depending on the medium conveying them. Fluids at rest, like the air, store for shorter durations of time the same information (a difference in temperature, for example) than those that have more inertia, such as water. This explains why differences in temperature are more important in ecosystem functioning for a continental climate than for a climate under an oceanic influence. A piece of information stored in a solid such as a rock is generally even more durable, as archaeologists and geologists know, but is probably more difficult to print. However, a piece of information can be long lasting in a fluid medium too if it is rewritten often.

For storing (information) for a long term, it follows that it is necessary either to store it in solid form, or to store it often. Life is the most beautiful example of the second option, and it shows that to do so, it needs a code (see Chapter 2). It is by encoding a piece of information and by developing at the same time a reading system (a decoder) that it becomes possible for it to be recopied and to acquire a certain degree of permanence. The appearance of language, and then of writing, has contributed greatly to preserving information. From this stored information, can flows start? The more stable the stored information and the more often it is read, the more frequent and numerous the flows. Our team analogy has a large number of encodings for the storing of information, and then for using it to contribute the working of the system. The first of these is the genetic encoding that shapes the driver and the other species that reside in it. Another encoding is the recipe that permits the construction of the vehicle (remember the cooking recipe of Chapter 2). This second encoding is not of the same type as the first, but it permits a storing of information about the arrangement and the interactions among the constituents of the vehicle. The third encoding is the human language that permits communication with the geolocation system regarding the team's location and the choice of ways to the desired destination. The other encodings, such as the Highway Code and handling rules of the vehicle, are as indispensable (though not always obvious) as the correct working of the team.

What does encoding mean? The word probably comes from the word codex that was used in the 13th Century to designate the boards used for writing, and by metonymy it soon began to mean the writing itself. According to the classical definitions, a code is a system of signs (for example icons or symbols) that, by convention, serve to represent and transmit information from a sender to a receiver. The property of transmissibility is particularly pertinent to what is of interest to us: it supports the concept of information flow between the components of ecosystems, between different media, that we have been seeking to highlight. The property of representation introduces a kind of semantics for information once encoded. We believe that if we can identify the codes in the ecosystem and understand their semantics, it will open a promising field of research.

The types of codes in ecosystems are certainly as numerous as those in the car-and-driver team of our analogy. Our mind turns immediately to the genetic information encoded in the metagenome. However, the genetic encoding exclusively relates to specific components (the biocoenosis, the human being, etc.), and its contribution to an understanding of the whole remains limited. The most natural idea would be to consider that ecosystemic information is also encoded in the structure of the relations that drive the ecosystem, that is the structure of its trophic and non-trophic networks (Frontier et al. 2008). The trophic network stores a great quantity of information about the interactions among the populations and individuals, and between the biocoenosis and the biotope. This network is stable enough in time, as long as it does not suffer a major disturbance. The trophic network is to the community a bit like what the DNA is to an individual. It leads each species in an ecosystem to where it ought to be in an ecosystem. The encoding of trophic information takes the form of a graph, the trophic graph. It is relational structure in a space of n dimensions, where n is the number of the species concerned that we usually project into a predation matrix in two dimensions (Figure 3.3).

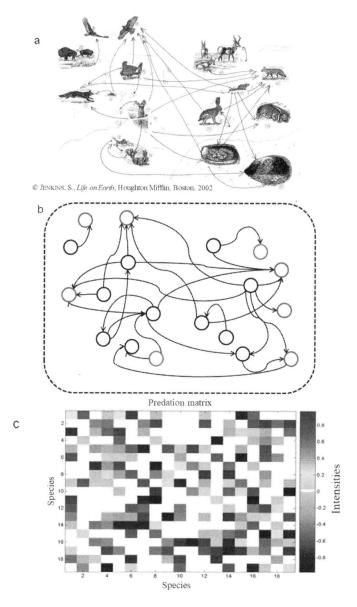

© JENKINS, S., *Life on Earth*, Houghton Mifflin, Boston, 2002

Figure 3.3. *A trophic network (a) is a graph connecting nodes and species, specifying those which feed on others. In another form, b) shows the predators in blue, herbivores in black, and primary resources in green. The network can be represented by a hypothetical predation matrix c), which specifies the intensity of predation between the 11 species. For a color version of this figure, see www.iste.co.uk/gaucherel/information.zip*

Of course, this trophic code misses the clarity and simplicity of the DNA molecule in its double helix. But an ecosystem is not an organism, and it is not usually circumscribed as a living entity. The ecosystem is a biological and physical entity that numerous internal and external couplings render complex to our eye. Nevertheless, the alphabet of the trophic code is still simpler than that of DNA with its four nucleotides. In its rudimentary version, it says: "Eat" or "Be eaten". Populations "read" this code naturally when they are confronted with populations of other species through the emergence of events of predation that materialize during encounters between individuals. All this happens as if the species read the information encoded by the two-letter code of the trophic graph (Figure 3.3).

Now how does this reading work? It is a bit like the board at a water fountain that tells us whether the water is potable or not. While we use our language to decode a syntagm ("Potable"/"Not potable"), that information could have been encoded in two values and would have produced two actions ("Drink"/"Don't drink"). An encounter between a lioness and an antelope could lead to a primarily binary event: eat or not eat. A placing of a pride of lions with a population of antelopes could have either of two values: eat (probably!) or to not eat (perhaps another population of prey is more accessible). Hence, the trophic code is decoded "internally" by the constituents of the ecosystem itself. This probably is why we have had so much difficulty detecting this decoding. The trophic graph is read locally by individuals and by the populations when they are placed together.

The decoding in this instance is not as obvious as in the case of DNA, largely so because it is not materialized by a specialized structure, for example the ribosome that serves the reading system in biological systems. The situation is clearly normal, and we should not expect ecosystemic code to resemble codes we already know. However, the trophic code that is proposed here covers the definition considered earlier: it represents and transfers information from an emitting component (resources and species) to a receptive one (predator species), or from the biotope to the biocoenosis. Anyhow, the species is to the trophic code what the molecule is to the genetic code.

This proposition separates the information carried by the trophic message through the encoding ("Eat"), on the one hand (the structure of the network), from that linked to the environment, on the other hand ("Eat if it is cold", for example). The distinction is as important as that which separates the genetic code from its reading system and the environment from its cell. There are several works on the trophic message. Some seek, for example, to understand the impact of the trophic structure on the stability of communities. According to Robert May, it appears that the community is unstable if the species are numerous or if the connectivity (the number of interactions) is high (May 1973). As we reduce these two parameters, we approach a frontier at which the communities appear stable. Most of the observed trophic networks occur on this frontier, proving that they approach a maximal complexity (in terms of connectivity and numbers of species) that keeps them stable. This observation remains an enigma, even if the self-organizing properties of the trophic networks could help provide a partial explanation.

Other networks of interactions in the ecosystem, which are numerous, do not function differently (Gaucherel *et al.* 2017). Their encoding resembles the trophic encoding, but their alphabet differs. A population may say "Help me"/"Don't help me", "Take advantage of me"/"Don't take advantage of me" or, more generally, "I mean a lot to you"/"I don't mean a lot to you", depending on whether we are dealing with symbiosis or amensalism or a possible absence of interaction. The weights and degrees of importance given to the encoded interactions in the trophic encoding are reminders of the expression of genes in their environment. As in the genetic case, the ecosystemic encoding and decoding exist, but the reading of the message depends highly on the environment in which it takes place (see Chapter 2). Note that the trophic encoding (the alphabet) remains the same for different ecosystems, but the structure of the network (the stored message) may differ systematically. The trophic graph stores different information coming from the same encoder/decoder system. It is this that unifies ecosystem functioning. We shall therefore name the encoding associated with these networks (trophic or non-trophic) *specific encoding*, because it places in a relationship all members among different populations and recalls the genetic encoding.

These specific networks are not immutable. Imagine yourselves in the Cambrian period, which lasted through a formidable explosion of diverse multicellular life some half a billion years ago. Geological data suggest a rise in the proportion of atmospheric oxygen at the time. Animals might have been able to benefit from the changes in the environment to develop a complex respiratory apparatus, grow their metabolism, and increase their size. As the temperature rose, they might have been able to diversify, perhaps at the cost of the animals from the pre-Cambrian period, either by competing with them or by predation. The appearance of numerous predators, capable of seeing and moving, no doubt introduced into these ecosystems a pressure to which the prey apparently responded with new means of protection (mineral exoskeletons) or new forms of behavior (burying themselves deeper in the sediments). Experts believe that predation and defense strategies developed during this turning point of life probably widened the Cambrian diversification. Many trophic networks therefore must belong to that ancient epoch, complexifying the specific coding with which it is associated.

Studying the networks that characterize the ecosystem as messages associated with a encoder/decoder system would allow us to envisage them in a new light: we might be able then to separate the information conveyed by the networks from the contingent material that produce them (the present populations) so as to better understand their dynamics and perhaps their origin. We shall for a moment put aside the trophic network, and concentrate on the encoding for this piece of information – on its semantic importance, in other words – on the whole possible set of messages rather on a particular (contingent) one. We may concentrate on the reading system, that is the decoder. Finally, we may study the extent to which this decoding is independent of the ecosystemic context, that is the environment. We may find again the three characteristics referred to in the previous chapters on language and biology, namely the message (M), added to which is the encoder/decoder (D) and the environment (E), which is home to and influences both. As we have said before in the case of the genetic instance, it is the MDE triad for which we should quantify the information, and not just for the message.

Ecosystemic codes, among others, are those that we have proposed to associate with interactions among species ("Eat" or "Not eat"). Their decoding is done by each population that reads a network of interactions at a given instant. The networks of interactions are the messages conveyed by the system. The networks use their structures, which change all the time, to freeze the relations among the populations, and decide how the community functions. Finally, the environment is the ecosystem as a whole (with the same ambiguity as for the organism at its approximately defined borders). Each MDE system defines a language. Some turn out to be at varying levels of efficiency in terms of permanence. The ecosystems we observe are resilient. The trophic encoding with its associated decoding allows the setting up of communities of robust species with regard to environmental changes. However, the ecosystems that lose or host certain key species may collapse or abruptly pass into a very different state: their trophic network and their functioning have changed.

We come back to some of the characteristics already identified in the biology of evolution. It is as if the ecosystemic information transfer, realized in different reading systems, had the effect of favoring the perpetuation of the ecosystem that it conveyed. This is not to say that ecosystems evolve, but there are great similarities between an organism and an ecosystem when one adopts an informational point of view.

The species network may thus be perceived in a purely informational way as a system that stores and decodes information. However, this view has the same simplistic character that we encountered in many instances in this chapter: the specific encoding concentrates on the biocoenosis, still in interaction with the biotope, but a biotope reduced to a minimalist component. It would have been better to bring out an encoding capable of recreating a more generic conceptual link among all the components of the ecosystem. The abiotic components of the ecosystem are underrepresented in the informational view we have presented, which suggests the existence of other encoding/decoding systems.

We may define another encoding of ecosystemic information, a still more hidden encoding: spatial heterogeneity. The spatial structures observed recurrently in ecosystems not only store information, but also encode it. When one component, say the faunal, encounters another component, say the floral, it is strongly constrained, even in its movements, and this has repercussions in the long term on its demography, and far more on its future speciations. The herbivores move on a grazing lawn. How do they decode the spatial information stored in the vegetal (and possibly soil) cover? A little like the way we decode road signals. The code here is simple: it says "Go!" (green) or "Stop!" (red). How is the information transferred from the floristic component to the faunistic? It takes place because of its heterogeneity that had stored beforehand a piece of spatial information. As it is well known in landscape ecology, the support structure restricts movements of the entity carried. The spatial encoding in this case is certainly not as clear-cut as this dual-color code may suggest and offers a broad palette of variations so gradual as to make it a spatial heterogeneity. What we are going to call spatial code is an analogical code. This spatial code is essential, because all movements in the world have constraints from their surrounding heterogeneities.

To summarize, the floral component contains certain information, information on heterogeneity. The ecosystem is also constituted of a spatial code that indicates to each of its components deployed in its space how it is to behave regarding to this spatial heterogeneity (it may or may not pass, be installed or not). The faunal component that encounters the floral component "reads" its information, which has been transferred to it because of the spatial code. The floral information is therefore "translated", then stored into a now faunal information. It will then interact with other information flows within the ecosystem.

Such a translation refers to some studies of the influence of landscape heterogeneity on the distributions of a population. We want to emphasize here the generality of the principle described at the informational level: there is a unity of functioning among the spatial, trophic, genetic and human properties of the ecosystem. More generally, we may retain the same logic while researching the encodings dedicated to the atmospheric and soil science components of the ecosystem whether we consider them abiotic or not. This unit of work will reappear in the information balance and the analysis of the identified encodings. A holistic (global) study of an ecosystem will help provide a better understanding of it, as the generic concept of encodings/decodings of information suggest. This preliminary interpretation holds out hopes for the working hypotheses that turn out to be useful to ecologists. We shall take up some of them in the following section, emphasizing the "languages" related to ecosystemic codes.

3.12. The languages of the ecosystem

These reflections, though attractive in helping understand the ecosystem, are far from offering a coherent ecosystemic theory. This interpretation and the search connected with it are still new. A major difficulty relates to bridging the physical and the biological concepts. Because of its genericity, the concept of information possesses the potential to reconcile the two fields if by chance we use it in studies of all the components of the ecosystem (biotic, abiotic, plus their interactions). That is why we believe that drawing up an information evaluation system, and identifying the languages of the ecosystems, would be the first step toward that objective. However, for a theory to be proposed, it is necessary to ensure that it should have some means of being refuted (that is, "falsifiable", in the words of Karl Popper, without forgetting the objections of that view). Here is a very incomplete list of testable hypotheses following naturally from the informational and linguistic point of views of ecosystems.

Before proposing working hypotheses, we must emphasize the dangers of going too far along the ecosystem/car-and-driver-team analogy that we used earlier. That analogy will have very limited value in the construction and testing of "linguistic" hypotheses in ecology. Some limitations will be obvious at once. Photosynthesis in ecology is not equivalent to the air-and-fuel explosion in a car's engine, and the motor is not a herbivore. The radio antenna is not a carnivore, even though it is placed far down the line in the energy-feeding network of the vehicle that supposedly mimics the trophic network. In every way, the vehicle, even while running, is not usually considered a living thing, contrary to what we supposed at times for the needs of illustration. We also visualized the driver stopping the vehicle and leaving it (which he would restart the next day). In fact, the biotic part of an ecosystem cannot be separated, even for a short while, from its abiotic part. This point justifies the indissociable interactions between the biocoenosis and the biotope. Despite these limitations, the car-and-driver metaphor would have been useful in whetting our interest in quantifying the flows and balance of information.

Let us return to the assumptions in the informational point of view of ecosystems and try to come up with some working hypotheses. To start with, it appears that an ecosystem tends by all means to persist. This assertion does not at all attribute an intention to the ecosystem; it merely propagates the biological principle of survival in the context of the ecosystem. Persisting here stands for stability across time in dynamic systems and not in the sense of resilience or robustness as C.S. Holling interprets the word (Holling 1973). The hypothesis does not preclude the possibility of the ecosystem changing drastically (due to disturbances, for example) in order to sustain itself over the long term. The ecosystem certainly does not reduce to a merely biological system; the many indices cited in this chapter persuade us to assume that the ecosystem is organized optimally or suboptimally to endure (as would a living organism) providing that it is as described at the informational level. The attempts already mentioned to demonstrate stability, homoeostasis or optimization within the ecosystem partly support this idea. If the optimization is proved in some cases, more work is still needed to show that it constitutes a rule. Numerous studies have shown the locally optimal character of some processes of the ecosystems – remember self-organization (Solé and Bascompte 2006). Our hypothesis aims to generalize this principle on the basis of an informational description. It is not a question of simply understanding how an ecosystem succeeds in stabilizing itself: it must also be shown that the ecosystem is locally the most stable possible.

Next, we may legitimately ask if the storing of information favors ecosystem sustainability. That implies that, total information (balance) being equal, the most stable ecosystem is the one best fixing the information flows that cross it. Although stored information will necessary last, it is a little harder to show that such a storing favors the perpetuation of the system. Models (analytical or numerical) will be valuable at this stage, for example, by simulating the same ecosystem with various storages and encodings. We might hope that, with ecological measures becoming more numerous, and the indices of complexity becoming more refined, we might succeed some day in quantifying this information for the ecosystems observed, and in identifying their most realistic simulations. We assume here that we know what to measure and how, which will form the central question in Chapter 4.

Third, the two preceding hypotheses might have applied only to purely physical systems. Now, the systems possess encodings that are their own, neither entirely physical nor entirely biological, as we have seen. Therefore, we ought to assume that an ecosystem encodes some information. This hypothesis lies at the heart of this chapter. Can we consider as encodings the influences of the spatial heterogeneity of an ecosystem or of its trophic and non-trophic alphabets? To answer the question, we will have to first characterize the encodings by formalizing the decodings under the form of languages, and then study the generality of the languages in large numbers of observed ecosystems, independently of the messages that they carry. Echoing the previous chapters, we shall emphasize the importance of qualifying and quantifying encoding information (and its environment information), more than just the messages, that they represent. The richness of the messages themselves is correlated to that of the encoding. Now how is one to quantify the richness of an ecosystemic encoding? And having seen that the ecosystemic encodings were numerous, which ones are the richest, the most changeable? Are they actually poorer than the genetic encoding or that of our linguistic grammars?

Encoding information improves its storage by permitting its reuse and persistence over time. The next stage would consist of assuming that the encoding of information enhances the longevity of the ecosystem. As Kolmogorov complexity tells us, duplicating a piece of information does not add (or only adds negligible) information to the previous situation. On the contrary, it only allows its spread to other places, at other moments, by other components of the ecosystem. This last hypothesis predicts that the perpetuation will be still better for several encodings, because the more the system encodes differently the more the information of different kinds it can store. This observation will cease to be true, of course, if the encodings are too redundant – but would this be the case for the encodings that we envisage for ecosystems? It is intuitive enough that an ecosystem contains more information, and more order, than an isolated organism. In some respects, it is also more complex. It contains in particular the genetic and biological information of the organism, plus the information of its relation with the other organisms in the ecosystem. These relations we believe are not completely encoded in genomes, as has been pointed out by Eva Jablonka and Marion J. Lamb in a recent book (Jablonka and Lamb 2005). Even if these events (the construction of an organism and its interactions with others) are not independent, this increase in information remains valid in quantitative terms. One way to test this hypothesis would be to model ecosystems hosting encodings of increasing complexity, and examine their stability over the long term, all other things being equal.

One hopes that the preceding hypotheses would have contributed toward explaining the functioning of an ecosystem. They postulate that the ecosystem seeks to exist, and that it has succeeded in doing so by encoding the information that flows through it. Much like life, which is rooted in genetic encoding, or our language that is very much encoded, these informational structures lead us inexorably toward more fundamental questions. They raise questions about the nature of these seemingly ubiquist encodings, questions Chapter 4 will take up by trying to redefine the concept of information and how to measure it.

4

Can We Define Information?

The previous chapters showed how pervasive the notion of information is in many aspects of life, from DNA molecules to ecosystems and human language. When seen from an informational perspective, these facets of life join in some form of unity that we will discuss in Chapter 5. Before that, we should manage to get a definition of information that covers the variety of situations that were evoked previously. Information is a rather recent scientific concept: it dates back to the middle of last century. Contrary to other well-established notions, information has not yet found its definitive definition. This chapter relies on some recent theoretical developments in algorithmic information theory that allow us to propose a common framework to describe the various situations we mentioned in which the word "information" occurred spontaneously.

4.1. Information as surprise

Any sign does not carry information. The oil level sensor in my car may invariably indicate level 7. If it could show only this value, the information associated with it would be zero. As we know that other values are possible, but are rare, the information attached to level 7 is very small. If the sensor indicates level 3 one day, the corresponding information that day will have a significant value.

In this example, one has clearly in mind what is at stake: the oil may be leaking. Let us forget about this for a while and concentrate on the sole probabilities. This is precisely what Claude Shannon did half a century ago. Shannon wanted to define information that travels through telecommunication networks to measure its useful rate (Shannon 1948). Quite counterintuitively at that time, he ignored any consideration relative to the semantics (meaning) of messages. The only preserved dimension in Shannon's theory is the probability of events. A rare event generates more information when it occurs than a frequent one. If one measures the probability of events by its equivalent in coin tosses, one gets (in bits) the amount of information that their occurrence generates. The occurrence of an event that has one in 1,000 chance of happening generates about 10 bits of information, as one has a one in 1,000 chance to get heads 10 times when flipping a coin 10 times. The occurrence of an event that has 50% chance of happening brings only one bit of information.

Information, as defined by Shannon, corresponds to the surprise caused by an event at the time of its occurrence. This surprise is measured by the *a priori* probability of the event. This definition requires not only the existence of an observer, but an observer who knows all alternatives in advance and who is able to assign a probability to each of them. Shannon's definition triggered a revolution in telecommunication technologies. Shannon was the first who understood that the effect of noise is not to degrade information, but merely to slow down its communication rate. His work gave rise to much excitement way beyond engineering communities. Quite naturally, biologists and thinkers in the social and human sciences made attempts to import the Shannonian notion of information into their own area with unequal success. Many criticized these efforts as simplistic (e.g. Griffiths 2001). This book, as it were, challenges these critiques.

We must acknowledge that a straightforward transposition of Shannon's definition of information outside of the strict area of coded transmissions may lead to absurd conclusions. Let us consider DNA. This long molecule (just consider that one DNA molecule may be several centimeter long, for a few millionths of a millimeter thick!) can be described as a string of pearls. These pearls are of four kinds, often represented by the four letters A, T, G and C (see Chapter 2). They are molecules that can bind to each other without preference for any order. A human chromosome may hold some 200 000 of them. How much information is there in one chromosome? Here, a computation of Shannon's concepts would give an absurd result: 200 million times the information of one single "pearl", that is 50 Mb. Why is this number absurd? Because it does not take into account the meaning contained in that DNA. It does not make any quantitative difference between that DNA and a random DNA sequence of the same length. Such a random sequence would have no chance of creating an organized being, whereas the information in our DNA was used to create us and can still be used to create our children. Intuitively, we can say that the human DNA contains information, whereas the random DNA sequence is mere noise and, with all due respect to Shannon, it does not contain any information whatsoever.

The gap between the intuitive notion of information and Shannon's definition widens when one takes average information, also called entropy, into account. Entropy is defined as the average value of information over all observed events (Delahaye 1994). Entropy is maximal when any redundancy has been eliminated. This makes sense. Any form of redundancy in a series of message provides indications about what will come next in that message, which diminishes the amount of information that can be expected from it. For instance, in this chapter, the character string "infor" is almost always followed by "mation" and conversely "mation" is almost always preceded by "infor". The presence of one string makes the occurrence of the other one certain. If we drop the "mation" suffix, the whole text will provide the same information with less characters and the average information, i.e. the entropy, would be reduced. This concept of entropy is understandably crucial in telecommunication technologies, as redundancy elimination leads to more efficient use of transmission channels. But again, when the concept of entropy is used to measure the average information content of a DNA sequence or of a book, seen as symbol sequences, it goes against intuition. A random sequence has maximal entropy, since it is unlikely to contain redundant sequences. By contrast, meaningful sequences, the DNA of a human being or the string of characters found in this book, include numerous redundancies such as the correlation between "infor" and "mation". When transposing the concept of entropy to this type of sequence, one reaches the absurd conclusion that they contain less information than random sequences of same length.

What can we do if the main standard definition of "information" fails so blatantly? First, we will observe that Shannon's principle of suppressing redundancy is worth pursuing. It is pushed to the extreme in the algorithmic theory of information. Second, we will reconsider Shannon's other idea that links information and surprise. This will lead us to a definition of information that can be applied to various contexts of interest.

4.2. Information measured by complexity

In the 1960s, three mathematicians, Ray Solomonoff, Andrei Kolmogorov and Gregory Chaitin, had the same idea independently. It consists of measuring the information content of an object by the size of its most concise exact summary (Delahaye 1994). This notion is called Kolmogorov complexity. A periodic string such as a-b-c-d-e-a-b-c-d-e-a-b-c-d-e-... is not complex at all, even it is several thousand letters long. It can be summarized by noticing that it results from the repetition of the pattern a-b-c-d-e. This pattern can itself be summarized by taking the first five letters of the alphabet; this is much more concise than having to specify five letters one by one among 26. Similarly, the famous number π is not complex at all. It can be reduced to a simple series: $\pi = 4 \times (1-1/3+1/5-1/7+1/9...)$. To retrieve π, we just need to form a series from the alternating inverse odd numbers and then multiply its sum by 4. It is somewhat simpler than enumerating the sequence of digits of π: 3-1-4-1-5-9-2-6-5-3-5-8-9-7-9-3-2-3-8-4-6-2-6-4-3-3-8-3-2-7-9-5... up to infinity. This approach to information is called algorithmic information theory, as the best summary of an object can be represented as the shortest algorithm (or computer program) that can generate that object.

This definition of information is in line with Shannon's idea of redundancy suppression, while carrying it to the extreme. Obviously, a very redundant series, such as a repetitive series, contains little information. It is also clear that the redundancy present in an object makes no contribution to its information content. By keeping only the gist of the object, Kolmogorov complexity measures useful information. The observer who perceives the object tries to summarize to the smallest possible size and infers from the result the quantity of information that the object contains. Information, in that sense, results from an operation of compression. For instance, people using a computer know that they can compress data. The most popular program to do this is certainly "Zip". Images are generally compressed before being stored or transmitted. Create an image with a painting software and then save it in a pixel format such as "gif". If your image is all white with only three black spots, the saved file will be much smaller than if your image is complex, with many intertwined points and lines. Even if the "gif" compression is far from being optimal, it illustrates the fact that the second image contains more information, in the sense of Kolmogorov, than the first image, which is simpler.

Contrary to Shannon's definition of information, the definition based on Kolmogorov complexity does not rely on previous knowledge of probability values. It does not require considering alternatives. It can be applied to unique objects, and not only to emitters that produce events repetitively with certain probabilities. No prior agreement is needed between an emitter and a receiver about the set of symbols that will be transmitted. This is good news if one wishes to consider data such as DNA, as there is no one that can say what is relevant to observe in that long molecule. The measure of complexity is not bound to focus on the occurrence of bases A, T, G, C or on codons, genes or gene groups. Any feature is good as long as it contributes to compressing the object (even if there is never any guaranty that optimal compression has been achieved). The algorithmic definition of information can even, in theory, get rid of any idea not only of emitters, but also of observers. Suffice it to say that all observers are equivalent: if one of them is able to summarize the object using an algorithm, that algorithm can be explained to any other observer. The algorithmic notion of information seems to reach an ideal status of objectivity.

Unfortunately, the algorithmic definition of information does not always match intuition. Randomness is the ultimate complexity. It is precisely this property that motivated Kolmogorov, Chaitin and others in their discovery of the concept of complexity. There is a perfect equivalence between being "random" and being "incompressible". But this beautiful correspondence is problematic in our context, as we fall back into the flaw mentioned about entropy: a random DNA molecule would be more complex than a human DNA molecule of the same length. By definition, the random molecule contains no redundancy that could be eliminated, leading to a shorter summary; it is maximally complex (note that the summary cannot merely mention the fact that the molecule is random, as the molecule has to be recoverable from the summary) (Delahaye 1994; Gaucherel 2014). On the other hand, any human DNA includes redundancies that would make a summary significantly shorter. We are back to square one: neither Shannon's definition nor the algorithmic complexity definition provides the intuition-matching notion of information that we need.

4.3. Information as organized complexity

Useful information seems to float between two extremes: extreme redundancy, as in a repetitive sequence, and extreme disorder, as in a random sequence. Shannon's entropy and Kolmogorov complexity are perfect tools to measure information by assessing the amount of redundancy. They are, however, unable to provide any safeguard against randomness.

Some authors suggested relying on another notion based on complexity and known as logical depth. This notion, introduced by Charles Bennett, aims at capturing the organized part of complexity that is neither too simple nor trivially random (Bennett 1988). Bennett is working at IBM Research. His idea is to consider not only the most concise summary of a given object, but rather the amount of time needed to reconstruct the object from that summary. The idea is appealing. This amount of time is small precisely for objects that our intuition considers devoid of information. A repetitive string such as a-b-c-d-e-a-b-c-d-e-a-b-c-d-e-... can be summarized by describing the repeated pattern. It is not deep within Bennett's meaning, as it can be quickly retrieved by copying the pattern. At the other extreme, a random sequence such as t-o-z-r-n-i-g-n-z-x-o-t-g-m-y-... cannot be summarized. In other terms, it constitutes its own summary. Between these two extremes, the string of letters that form the present book is slightly more complex within Bennett's meaning: it can be compressed by eliminating its redundancy (without loss of information), but the converse operation may take some time.

Quite understandably, some authors such as Jean-Paul Delahaye are tempted to use logical depth to measure the information "content" of living beings (Delahaye 1994; Dessalles 2010). It is clear that our DNA is a good summary of a significant part of us. This molecule includes most of what twins have in common, which is quite something. The way people look as individuals can be "compressed" to such a large extent that their DNA, represented as a string, can be stored on a mere CD-Rom. For Delahaye, humans are deep under Bennett's definition, because it is impossible to construct them quickly from their DNA. The only known way is to perform all operations that occur during embryogenesis.

The notion of logical depth captures another form of complexity, i.e. "organized" complexity. Engineers can probably think of a procedure to assemble a car in such a way that its different parts are built up in a parallel way. The architecture of a car is not that deep. A biological being has to be functional at each step of its development. This excludes the possibility of it being assembled piece by piece. Its organization is as complex as it is for a computer processor, which requires hundreds of operations to be performed in a strict order.

Kolmogorov complexity corresponds to the size of the object after it has been compressed. Logical depth, or organized complexity, takes decompression time into account. The latter notion is interesting and has not yet been fully explored. One of its drawbacks in our context, however, is due to the fact that it breaks the link, introduced by Shannon, between information and surprise or, in other terms, between information and low probability. In reality, the same objection can be addressed to Kolmogorov complexity. It is, however, easy to reconcile Shannon's information and Kolmogorov complexity, as we see in the following.

4.4. Information as compression

Shannon's idea was to define information from the receiver's perspective in a transmission scenario. The receiver detects signals, considers their *a priori* probability and deduces the amount of information that has been transmitted. This approach proves insufficient in our context. To keep the idea that information measures a certain amount of surprise, we need two points of view. Surprise results from a disparity: it corresponds to the gap between expectation and observation. Information is not an absolute quantity, but a difference between two values.

If we apply this principle to the algorithmic approach to information, absolute complexity does not matter. What matters is the difference between two complexity values, measures from two different points of view. This summary between Shannon's idea of surprise and Kolmogorov complexity leads to a new definition of information that will prove useful in many contexts that we will consider (Dessalles 2013). Kolmogorov complexity measures the end result of an ideal compression; we will measure information by the amplitude of that compression. Let us consider a few examples.

A first illustration of the principle information is that compression is offered by what we, humans, regard as interesting. For human beings, information coincides with what elicits their interest (see Chapter 1). Suppose that a fire broke out. This is an event, i.e. a unique situation that can be distinguished from any other by its date, its location, the people involved and the occurence that took place. With this definition, every event is certainly unique. Among the hundreds of daily experiences, very few are interesting, narratable events. To be interesting, an event must only be unique (which it obviously is), but it must also be peculiar. A situation is peculiar if it is unique for a simple reason. We hear quite often about fires in the news. The typical place for a blaze is complex: such and such district in Paris, such and such hotel in a town we do not exactly know. If the news tells us that the blaze occurred in the Eiffel Tower, as was the case on July 22, 2003, the location turns out to be simpler than expected. The event is easily characterized, at least more easily than expected. The difference corresponds to a compression, which generates information. The same thing applies if the blaze occurred in a celebrity's property or near your home. In each case, the simplicity of the place leads to a drop in complexity, i.e. compression. The event becomes peculiar.

On October 16, 2010, the Israeli lottery announced the following draw: 13-14-26-32-33-36. Most people did not play, so they did not detect any information there. Yet, exactly the same combination of numbers had been drawn 3 weeks earlier, on September 21. The news got formidable importance and was even reported in foreign newspapers. This makes sense if one realizes that the event offers significant compression. Usually, the minimal designation of the draw of the day requires enumerating the six drawn numbers. There is no compression. But on that day, a much more concise description was available. It consisted of indicating a rank in the list of past draws. Only one number is required, instead of six, so five numbers are spared. Once converted into bits, the difference measures the value of the information (if one ignores the cost of designating the concepts required from the context: lottery + Israel + date). The same principle of compression is at work to explain why a draw like 1-2-3-4-5-6, if it ever occurred, would be fantastic news even for those who did not play.

The previous examples are about peculiar situations with nothing at stakes for the observer. An expression like "the value of information" is ambiguous. If you hope for a bonus of €10,000 that only two candidates can receive, the information that you got it is worth only 1 bit, while the stakes are measured in thousands of euros. Here, we will restrict the word "information" to its meaning as a compression or complexity drop, ignoring what is at stakes. Note that it is crucial for journalists to include the stakes in order to anticipate the emotional impact of reported events on the readership. To do so, compression can be converted into probability (each bit corresponds to flipping a coin, i.e. probability 1/2; two bits, two coin tosses, probability 1/4; and so on), and then multiplied by the stakes to get the emotional intensity of the event.

Could we transpose the definition information = compression to contexts that are not specific to human communication? When an event is perceived by human beings, they expect a level of complexity that depends on their knowledge of the world, for instance the complexity of producing a lottery draw, and they observe a lower level complexity after the fact. Information can be measured by the difference between these two complexity levels. More generally, any information generates a complexity drop relative to a certain aspect of the world for a given observer. What about animals?

Let us see, for instance, whether the definition applies to the bee dance (see Chapter 1). A bee worker that is waking up and decides to go foraging must first choose which direction to fly. Her choice is complex: if she may choose among about 100 different directions, the complexity of her decision amounts to 7 bits. This corresponds to seven tosses of a coin, because with seven successive binary choices, one can reach up to 128 possibilities. If, instead of picking a flight direction randomly, she decides to read the direction from her sister's dance, the complexity of her decision drops down to zero: the flight direction is included in the dance, there is nothing left to do to determine it. Our bee got an amount of information that corresponds to the complexity drop, here 7 bits. If she hesitates between two dancers, her decision still requires 1 bit. The amount of compression is now only 6 bits. Note that there is indeed a double perspective: before and after consulting the dancer.

Can we use the complexity drop notion to characterize the amount of information contained in the human DNA? It all depends on the (double) point of view adopted. One may initially see only a random sequence in that DNA, and then observe that it is nothing like random as it can guide the synthesis of many molecules, including the 20,000 different proteins that our cells may contain. The corresponding complexity drop gives one measure of the information included in our DNA, a value up to 750 Mb. But we can adopt a totally different pair of viewpoints. The investigator who finds DNA on a crime scene may have no idea about its owner. They must discriminate among 6 or 7 billion possible individuals, which gives a complexity of 33 bits (if they think that the suspect must be male and French, 25 bits are still needed to determine him). Once the DNA has been analyzed and the culprit is identified, complexity drops down to 0. For the investigator, the amount of information contained in the DNA amounts to 33 bits (or 25 bits in the French case), much less than for the biologist. Note that the requirement of complexity drop confers zero information to a random DNA sequence, as intuition dictates. This problem, which proved insurmountable when adopting Shannon's definition or the classical complexity definition, does not exist anymore.

Information, according to the definition considered here, depends on an adjustment taking place by the observer. The observed situation is now more compact than before (Dessalles 2013). This applies to an observer who considers a situation and can now see a structure that went unnoticed before. This structure provides information, inasmuch as it offers a mode concise description of the situation. According to Gregory Chaitin's famous aphorism, "comprehension is compression". Note that within this logic, a scientist who makes sense of a phenomenon creates information.

4.5. Coding and information reading

As users of recent new technologies, we have no problem associating information, not only to the network on which it is circulating, but also to the devices on which it is stored. The hard disk in our computer contains what we regard as information. It contains, for instance, the buying date of the TV set that just broke down and that is perhaps under guarantee. Information must be stored or it disappears. If information, as claimed before, corresponds to a complexity drop, what is stored in memory?

According to the definition, information only exists in the eye of the observer who interprets it. Saying that information is stored is therefore misusing language. The permanent material medium on which memory is recorded, be it silicon, synapses or DNA, is no more than a precondition of information. Information only exists by the time of interpretation. Stored data must be read for information to be produced. In addition, the reading has to generate simplification for the entity that performs the reading. In many cases, interpretation amounts to mere decoding, but this is not always the case.

A reading device can detect the signs that have been recorded on some material substrate (paper, silicon, magnetic layer, bumps on an optical disc, synapses, DNA molecule, etc.). These signs only become information when the device is able to decode them. Your visual system perceives ink marks on the paper; it is able to transform them into letters, then into words and sentences. At each step, decoding occurs and information is created. A decoder is like the foraging bee of our example. It expects to read one printed character among 100 (including upper and lower case, digits, accents and punctuation). The complexity of its decision amounts to 7 bits. Once it has recognized a character, complexity drops by 7 bits. Seven bits of information have been created. A Chinese reader who would not know about the Latin alphabet would not have created this information. Written signs constitute potential information. Its amount can be quantified by the agent who wrote them down on the material substrate. These signs become actual information only when they are read and decoded.

Codes establish a correspondence that is known in advance by the observer between two domains, a sign space and a meaning space (see Chapter 1). A reader who understands English can decode characters, words and sentences from the present text because she knows the alphabet, the lexicon and the grammar of this language. Another example in which several codes are at work is offered by molecular biology. DNA elements (the base pairs), once transformed into RNA, are read three by three as codons (Chapter 2). The ribosome and its adjuncts that read the RNA operate as a decoder (Rana and Ankri 2016). At each step, 21 possibilities are offered, as the repertoire of meanings includes 20 amino acids and one "stop" instruction. The ribosome that selects the right t-RNA sees complexity drop from some 4.4 bits to 0 bits. Each codon brings more than 4 bits of information. The decoding process does not stop there. If we draw an analogy with language, DNA base pairs correspond to phonemes and amino acids to words. Words are assembled to form sentences; likewise, amino acids are assembled to form proteins. Sentences build up discourse; likewise, proteins build up biological structures (for instance the cytoskeleton of our cells) or chemical reaction cycles (for instance the Krebs cycle that allows our cells to generate energy). Biological combining goes further up, as it includes cells, organs, organisms, societies, species and ecosystems.

These two interpretation hierarchies, the linguistic and the biological ones, use combinatorial codes (Chapter 1). The signs at work at one level result from a combination of meanings decoded at the level below. Sentences are combinations of words, and proteins are combinations of amino acids. If one draws the analogy between language and biology further up, one is confronted with the issue of the nature of meaning. When we read a text, we give meaning to words, then to sentences, then to discourse. At which step of their development do the molecules get their meaning?

In principle, any information has meaning. In the case of language, however, the word "meaning" is used for the upper layers of interpretations, where we build images and attitudes (Tournebize and Gaucherel 2016). The meaning of a sentence like "the carpet is gray" is not yet generated when the letters c-a-r-p-e-t are put together and when the word "carpet" is recognized. Meaning only begins to appear when we form a perceptive representation of the sentence, when we figure out which carpet is concerned and when we form an attitude: disappointment, satisfaction and surprise (we asked for a red carpet; gray carpets do not show the dirt; all carpets are red in the building, but this one). Note that at these upper levels, meaning is not decoded, but computed. Information does not result from mere systematic matching, but requires interpretation and context.

By analogy with language, we may use the word "meaning" to refer to situations in which information requires interpretation to be produced. This means that the reading device, when producing information, carries out non-trivial computations that take context into account. Biology provides a variety of examples in which talking about "meaning" is not far-fetched. When biologists began to understand the genetic code, they naturally thought that protein synthesis consisted of mere systematic matching with chunks of DNA: one gene equals one protein. Reality, in eukaryotes, is quite different. Eukaryotic genes are not decoded. They are interpreted by the cell machinery (see Chapter 2). In its simple form, the mechanism goes like this: a gene is translated into an m-RNA, which is itself translated into a protein. Between these two phases, however, the mRNA may undergo a variety of splicing and editing operations that depend on the presence of other molecules in the cell nucleus, in particular small specialized RNA molecules that result themselves from transcriptions of other regions of the DNA (Chapter 2).

Because of this complex machinery that depends on context, we can say that the cell interprets genes and give them meaning. In context A, a gene is read in a certain way and gives rise to the synthesis of a protein, P1, which is likely to be appropriate to that context. In a different context B, the gene will be interpreted in another way and produces another protein, P2, which is adapted to B, since the cell evolved for this. The meaning of the gene may be P1 or P2, depending on the context. A sentence such as "the flower is in the book" may mean in a certain context that the flower is drawn on a page of the book or, in another context, that a dried flower has been inserted between two pages of the book. The cell genetic machinery in eukaryotes interprets genes as we do for sentences of our language.

The genetic reading system has a unique feature: it is in a situation in which it decodes itself. Molecules that support the interpretation of the genome, for instance the molecules that make up the ribosomes, are themselves coded in the genome and the corresponding genes must be interpreted by ribosomes for these molecules to exist. This circularity is nothing shocking, conceptually. Computer science offers an analog situation. Typical computer programmes must be compiled by a specialized program, called a compiler, to be executed. If the program is written in Java, one needs a Java compiler. But since the compiler is itself a computer program, nothing prevents us from writing it in Java. Such a compiler can execute any Java program, including the one that brought it into existence. It is a case of self-interpretation, as in the case of the ribosome that interprets genetic instructions and generates a new, fully identical, ribosome. In the compiler case, however, the self-interpretation is not material by nature. The only hardware is provided by the computer circuits that remain unchanged. The biological machine is the only one that is known to interpret itself, including at the hardware level. If one day we ever produce robots that, using soldering irons and pliers, can make many things including material copies of themselves, the situation will have changed.

4.6. Memory

By decoding information, observers lower the complexity of their choice or of what is to be remembered. In this sense, information leads to compression. An entity that requires no information to work is a simple automaton that achieves only one task. As a whole, a bacterium looks at first sight like such a simple automaton, as it manages to duplicate in a variety of environments, with no significant change in the result. Yet, like our computers, and even like human individuals who build up their beliefs, the bacterium has potentialities that go way beyond what it eventually achieves. We can verify this easily nowadays: we ask bacteria to produce proteins that are unknown in the bacterial world, such as human insulin, and they do it willingly. For an engineer, the normal functioning of a bacterium looks like a fantastic waste, as if an ultra-powerful computer was used for one single deterministic task such as printing always the same sentence.

This impression is wrong and results from an illusion. We see the (simplified) bacterium in our example as an informationally closed system, because it does not seem to extract much information from its environment during its life. But even in its standard functioning that seems so mechanical, the bacterium gets information from its genome. This information was transmitted to it by its mother bacterium (we ignore here all other genetic transfers that operate in the bacterial world). Memory is an information transfer that operates through time rather than through space (Suddendorf and Corballis 2007). Our genes are messages that were sent to us by our far ancestors and that we are sending to our descendants, if we choose to have some.

Human beings, as compared to other primates, have overdeveloped memory capacities. The major part of their disproportionate cortex is not devoted to making elaborate computations. With a few exceptions, mostly linked to language, the kind of computations that our brain carries out are similar to those that a chimpanzee brain does. The most complex ones are probably associated with processes involved in shape recognition in dynamic environments. The reason why our cerebral mass has increased threefold from our last common ancestor with chimpanzees has more to do with the storing function. Our episodic memory is able to store thousands of life experiences in great detail. We store events that we regard as information, i.e. peculiar situations. Most of these situations are futile from a biological point of view, which means that they have no consequence regarding our life expectancy or our reproduction. Moreover, they are so peculiar that they are highly unlikely to occur ever again. It is even their singularity that induced their memorization. Why is it so? The primary objective of episodic memory is not to store a huge repertoire of specific situations from which we would draw at each moment to pick appropriate behavior (Suddendorf and Corballis 2007). Animals do without such a system that, besides, would be rather inefficient. Most of the time, our daily actions do not result from merely copying past models of action that we would have memorized to reproduce. The primary function of episodic memory is quite different. This human speciality has to do with the narrative function of language (Dessalles 2007a). If we can remember so many peculiar situations, it is to retell them to others during the innumerable story rounds that fill up a good part of our daily language activities. The function of our memory is to make a delayed transmission of information possible. When we experience a peculiar event, our instinctive reaction is to draw attention to it or to tell others about it. This leads our interlocutors to experience the complexity drop attached to the peculiar character of the event by themselves. Our episodic memory is no more than a go-between that allow us to reach interlocutors further through time.

Similarly, the genetic material in our cells or in viruses constitutes a delayed information transmission. Because of this information, the cell machinery can reduce the complexity of its choices. The cellular interpretation device is ultra-powerful. Our machines did not need much information to work until the computer era. The cell machinery is like our computers. It can do "everything". It uses the information it gets through time from genetic memory to make its choices considerably less complex. Without the possibility of memorizing information, life would be confined to the temporality of dynamic systems. The material recording of information, in texts, in neurons, in molecules or in the physical environment, opens up new possibilities for living beings to travel through time.

5

Evolution of Information

It was some 40 years ago that biologist François Jacob concluded his book "The Logic of Life" with this sentence (Jacob 1993): "Today the world is messages, codes, and information". We have tried to illustrate this intuition. We have confirmed and shown the crucial role of information and its encoding in the working of the world around us. It is, of course, possible that our approach has not taken the correct direction. We started off with code because it appeared to be the most obvious choice, and the most intuitive. After all, we humans use it all the time in the form of language. For as long as *Homo sapiens* has existed, and in all human cultures, people have recognized the importance of words and their association with ideas and things. The second code that we considered, namely genetic code, only appeared half a century ago. In fact, genetic code has been around for billions of years, and is perhaps 15,000 times older than the language that we use to communicate. Analysis of ecosystems and of the entities acting on codes as well as storage of information is still more recent than the discovery of genetic code. However, the phenomenon that it describes may indeed be much older than all else. Is it possible that the role of information in living systems is solely a tiny fragment of reality? It seems as if the chronology of our discoveries concerning information in life sciences, and, therefore, the chronology of this book, have both been in a direction opposite to the direction of the chronology of the strides the world has made.

5.1. In the beginning was structure

In Chapter 4, we suggested that in order to be able to measure information in a given context, one would begin by observing and evaluating the reduction in complexity in it. Typical instances of a lowering in complexity are linked to the detection of a structure. When one among us notices an analogy between two situations, those two situations form a coherent structure (even if this is fortuitous), and we then instinctively talk about it to our fellow researchers. Given such a definition, can information exist without a human observer? We answer in the affirmative. When a tRNA specifies its preferred codon, it creates a piece of information. The codon plays the role of the structure detected and the tRNA the role of the observer. The tRNA is itself a structure, but a structure of particular type. It is a *structure sensitive to structure*, and we shall designate such a structure with the acronym SSS. According to our definition, therefore, a structure exists if, and only if, there exists an observer or an SSS capable of detecting it. It is a corollary that information is as old as the SSSs.

We have seen that the living world is overflowing with SSSs: anticodons, microRNAs, proteins, networks of biochemical reactions and so forth. Ecosystems may be analyzed equally well from the angle of the SSSs. To illustrate this point, a species constitutes a structure capable of "reading" a trophic network. As a foreign entity when it entered the ecosystem, its entry depended on the structure of the preexisting trophic network (Gaucherel *et al.* 2017). Since its structure is determined by its strength, its feeding behavior and its occupation of space, the species qualifies to be classed as an SSS. If this analysis is valid, it may lead us back to a point in time when genetic code had not yet come into being.

There are multiple hypotheses as to when life first appeared on Earth. However, if we were to omit those that cling to an extraterrestrial origin for the first cells, we would notice that these hypotheses often share the idea of a prebiotic "soup" in which molecules capable of catalyzing their common syntheses ranged over increasingly complex structures, simply by means of random physicochemical combinations. Prior to this scenario, there were perhaps different mineral structures, among them crystals that explored autocatalysis after the Earth's crust froze. In a biochemical approach, such a molecule stabilizes, catalyzes, metabolizes or destroys another molecule, and the first SSSs are then born on Earth. If we were to follow this line of reasoning, information is seen to be born in the primordial soup, even before the arrival of a self-replicating system. The first codes (whether to catalyze or not, to metabolize or not) were short lived, far shorter in duration than genetic code. They only lasted for as long as the populations of the molecules involved in the network of physicochemical affinity relationships occupied the same place, in the same pool, or in the same early mud as before.

Nevertheless, we owe our lives to these codes. The complexification of prebiotic physicochemical relationships would only have been possible if nature was able to construct the complexity step by step. We might describe each of these steps by their constituent structures, in this specific case the chemical species and the physical structures. A reduction such as this (if it were possible) would not by itself explain the sequence of events. If we were to follow the information approach, every single step should then be characterized by the relationships among the SSSs. Our message–decoder–environment (MDE) scheme is already at work, with the first SSSs playing the role of decoder, while the structure to which the SSS is sensitive plays the role of message, and the relationships among the SSSs constitute the (essential) environment. The existence of these relationships allows us to compare the systems of the SSSs that coexist with languages. From this perspective, what then was nature's first language?

5.2. The first languages were ecosystemic

We considered in Chapter 1 the different characteristics that a language must possess. A language might be analog or digital, holistic or combinatory, referential, arbitrary, compositional and it may have a syntax. We also suggested the existence of a relationship among these attributes: a digital code comes typically from an analog code after quantification and simplification; an iconic code can derive from a code of an arbitrary language; a combinatory code is a product of the fragmentation of a holistic code (see Figure 1.10). We therefore expect that, chronologically, the first language of nature was analog, holistic, non-arbitrary and without syntax. Ecosystemic languages, from this point of view, seem suitable candidates for this position (see Chapter 3).

The relationships that existed among the first SSSs of prebiotic Earth may be considered to have been of an ecosystemic nature that included, in particular, the processes of consumption (this takes place when one chemical species damages another) and inhibition (a phenomenon occurring when one chemical species creates conditions that are unfavorable to another species). Prebiotic nature "spoke" through the codes mentioned previously. This was quite similar to how present-day ecosystems are seen to behave when looked at from the perspective of information. The properties of ecosystemic code appear to us to be analog: predation, symbiosis, parasitism and spatial presence are essentially gradual in nature, when viewed from the level of the populations. The codes, such as are "read" by the populations, are holistic, and each code stands for a single unit of meaning. We should consider these codes as being non-arbitrary: the connection between the information in the phrase "is eaten by" and its decoding in terms of the insertion of a species into an ecosystem, or in terms of demographics, is a necessary connection, and not an arbitrary one. Therefore, it is not surprising that, in an information-based perspective of life, analog, holistic and non-arbitrary codes of the ecosystemic kind have taken precedence over all the others.

Information that travels through codes such as these influences its own future. Relations such as "who eats whom" or "what releases what" have effects on predation or movements on the subsequent stages of the ecosystem's life (Frontier *et al.* 2008; Gaucherel *et al.* 2017). The appearance of the first self-replicating systems has changed everything by opening the way to a new form of language, with a digital code.

5.3. The replicators and the conservators

The appearance of the SSSs opened up new possibilities. Some SSSs' structures are sensitive to other SSSs. These structures may form information sequences in which each link is detected by the following one. If the environment allows the sequences to multiply, the networks of interaction inevitably appear to be cycles. A cycle can become self-destructive. To take a simple example, if A allows B to exist, and B destroys A, then both run the risk of disappearing together, or at least that of inducing the existence of C who himself/herself produced A. The evolution of cycles depends in a complex manner on the totality of the reactions involved.

Yet, some cycles may have simple effects, such as stabilizing the structures that constitute them (and thus stabilizing themselves) or even favoring a replication of their components. These two phenomena give rise to a selective process. We observe structures that are, with the greatest probability, included in self-stabilizing or self-replicating cycles. In other words, except for transitory phases, the structures that prevail are those that are capable of persisting as unique structures or collections of copies while constantly changing their components. We will label as *replicators* those structures that create copies of themselves either directly or indirectly, and as *conservators* those that belong to a self-stabilizing cycle.

The molecules in the DNA double helix have a self-replicating property, while they also bring about the synthesis of numerous structures, such as ribosomes and DNA polymerase that in turn directly or indirectly facilitate DNA replication (Pray 2008; Danchin *et al.* 2011b). The cycle can be long. DNA controls the structure and function of a cell that is involved in a system which it inhabits to divide and thus replicate the initial DNA. The DNAs present on present-day Earth are those that belong to the most effective cycles in terms of sustainability. The theory of natural selection, proposed in the 19th Century by Charles Darwin and Alfred Wallace, says exactly that, clarifying that new players constantly appear through variations (such as mutations).

A similar argument could be made for ecosystems. If we accept that ecosystems are made up of structures sensitive to other structures, we should expect cycles. The ecosystemic structures one sees are therefore, and with even greater probability, those that are capable of stabilizing themselves. A predator–prey system in two species will move back and forth unsteadily, leading to a possible extinction of the predator species (Lindeman 1942; Gaucherel *et al.* 2017). A more complex trophic network, with cycles (such as those in which the prey consumed the predator's young or corpse), can achieve stability, and endure by marginally adapting to species that may appear in the system or disappear.

Replicators and conservators endure across time. Their components, namely molecules, cells and individuals, have relatively short lives, dissolving into their elementary components at the end of their term. Our body is a conservator that constantly changes its constituent atoms. According to the Gaia hypothesis developed in the 1970s by James Lovelock and Lynn Margulis (Lovelock 2000), our planet is a conservator-type ecosystem: for instance, using the cycle of the carbon sometimes trapped in limestone deposits, and sometimes released in the form of carbon dioxide or methane, it keeps its temperature and the composition of its atmosphere within the margins compatible with life, even if life keeps changing. The successful cultural "memes" (see Chapter 1) may be considered replicators, sometimes able to survive in a culture for centuries, well beyond the lifetime of the human brains that host them.

Replicators and conservators are not physical entities, even though they are only realized in a physical form, despite the fact that they survive in their components. We ought to regard them as being in the nature of information. Physical structures do not survive across time; information does.

This description in terms of replicators and conservators stands in contrast with the descriptions of nature in terms of dynamic systems that were made popular by Francisco Varela (Varela *et al.* 1974). The two descriptions can be regarded as representing two perspectives of the same reality, each with its own orientation. One instance of this would be the description of natural phenomena in which information is quantified, and another that deals with codes and languages. Just as it may be desirable to consider the working of a computer in terms of programs, and not only in terms of electric currents, it seems sensible to show that life has the ability to manage information according to codes and languages at all levels, even though this is a statement that needs to be explained in some detail. While dynamical systems use an approach based on trajectories and attractors in the space of variables, the replicators and conservators may look like "information attractors" (to preserve the analogy of dynamical systems). Quite simply, their encoded description occupies a level that is more global than the level of the kinetics of change. This approach makes intelligible what endures beyond all contingent changes.

The "information attractors" are purely local. Unlike the attractors of physical systems, these are contingent: they are a product of history. They are attractors only because of their permanence and their resilience if they are conservators, and because of their ability to endure across generations if they are replicators. As long as they are adapted to their environment, they will not be affected by most disturbances or mutations. Now, what does "adapted" mean in this context?

We might say that, in a manner of speaking, an information attractor channels the information that defines it. We might even propose the idea that it does so by locally maximizing the information flow that goes across time. For example, replicators that are adapted are those whose effect on the environment maximizes their own replication. Those that ensure a maximal propagation of information are those that we observe, since they outperform the less efficient replicators with whom they are in competition. Similarly, the components of an ecosystem, regardless of whether it is biotic or abiotic, if they persist, are such that the information they provide to the rest of the system favors their own sustainability. Then again, we expect that the sustainability is more likely to succeed if the information flow is maximum. This idea, while true in some cases, still represents an interesting conjecture.

5.4. Biological languages

What we have just said about information flow may also be said about codes. We may speak of language when the SSSs are organized into a system. For example, different tRNAs recognize different structures (codons), and they work together during the synthesis of a polypeptide chain (Chapter 2), and we may well speak of genetic language in this context. The set of tRNAs defines a language that has the properties of being digital and combinatory.

Decoding is a process that rolls out in time and conditions the system's future states, setting it to work, or, to use a language metaphor, we may say that the system has literally sent a message to its future. In the case of genetic language, the message is sent to the future of the organism during development as well as to future generations.

We might expect that the codes enabling the best information flows dominate. These are not necessarily the codes that are the most complex: the code and the type of information concerned are to be adapted to one another if they are to work. Consider again the example of genetic code.

Old conceptions of heredity were of the analog type. One's form at birth was supposedly modeled on the parents, a bit like a copy of an original. We might imagine that on another planet a different form of life had arrived, say, for example, two-dimensional beings that could only reproduce like photocopies: each element of the surface would attract a similar element to the two-dimensional duplicate up to the time that it was ready to separate from the mother matrix. Life on Earth has not followed this course (if we exclude certain aspects of epigenetics), or, if it did, that form of life died out and made way for the form of life that we know, the one that is based on digital heredity (see Chapter 2). Biochemical replicators do appear able to pass down time until they achieve perfect copies that only digital code can make possible. In this case, we may say that the code itself was selected.

5.5. Information selection

Replicators and conservators are not perpetual entities. Their survival is dependent on the narrow domain in which they operate. When the system of which they are elements leaves the domain, for whatever reason, these structures disappear. The structures of an ecosystem do not survive if a large proportion of species disappear, an eventuality that is locally possible at any time, and actually occurred on Earth during the five great extinction episodes. The main cause of the disappearance of replicators and conservators, however, lies elsewhere. The finger points to the fact that replicators and conservators are in competition with their alleles.

We shall label as an allele of a replicator or of a conservator a structure with which they are incompatible. In genetics, two alleles of the same gene occupy the same place on the chromosome, but two alleles cannot be present on the same DNA molecule. The allele of a spatial network in an ecosystem corresponds to all the other spatial networks involving the same species, but with different locations, obstacles and transitions. It occurs when a population is divided into two by a mountain chain or a separation of continents. The allele of a cultural meme corresponds to all other cultural memes with which it is incompatible (for example believing that Elvis Presley is dead, and believing that he is still alive). The perpetuity of replicators and conservators inevitably puts them in competition with their alleles. If one of these alleles dominates, it is to the detriment of the others which are therefore doomed to extinction.

In the 1960s, John H. Holland described evolution as a contest among allelic schemata (Holland 1975). In this context, a schema is a partial specification of the genome: certain sites of the genome are looked at, and elements of interest specified. For instance, a schema may specify that the bases T, C and C exist on three particular sites, not necessarily contiguous. This schema possesses 63 allelic schemata that specify for the same three positions TCA, TCT, TCG, TAC, etc. Holland described evolution as a process that had the effect of sorting allelic schemata. Individuals die, but the schemata live on for generations. Evolution, while assessing individuals, indirectly assesses their schemata. The adaptive value of a schema obviously depends on the context, that is, on the presence of other (non-allelic) schemata specifying other positions of the genome. The schemata that we observe are those that, in the context of other schemata, have succeeded in imposing themselves at the expense of their allelic schemata.

Holland's schemata are an example of a typical replicator. The idea was reprised by Richard Dawkins in his "selfish gene" metaphor (Dawkins 1976). Unlike the vague idea of the gene that sometimes designates a functional segment of DNA encoding a protein, the notion of schema only retains the information aspect. Replicators that succeed in the play of evolution transmit whatever constitutes their difference with others. Therefore, a schema is the quintessence of a replicator, since it only contains what makes the difference.

The contextual character of the adaptation of schemata makes it possible to accord a positive role to the environment (the "E" in the MDE system). The working of a functional entity, seen as a decoder, cannot be thought of in isolation. We have to take account of the context, starting with the organisms that the environment shelters. A description in terms of alleles explains why the environment, far from being just a troublemaker, shapes the entire surrounding in which decoding becomes possible. The metaphor of the car-and-driver team in Chapter 4 provides an illustration of this. While different persons may occupy the seat of the driver, only one can actually be the driver at a given point in time. A proper performance of the driving task depends on him or her, for example depending on whether he/she is an adult or a child. It also depends on other variables, alleles in this context: if the driver suffers from a leg injury, driving will be easier with the accelerator positioned close to the steering wheel instead of on the floor of the vehicle.

Let us take another metaphor, this time from the domain of music. The role of each allele, whether genetic, ecological, even cultural, or of another sort, resembles the sound of an instrument that is able to play one note at a time. The entity that hosts the alleles resembles an orchestra in which each instrument is the source of a combination of notes. Evolution corresponds to a search for a "harmonious" chord composed of the possibly disparate notes. The global setting not being immutable, what results is a rendering made up of a suite of chords separated by transitions. Nature's information-based approach consists of describing the score that creates this music and the rules of harmony that control it by ignoring characteristics of detail, such as the material of which the instruments were made.

5.6. Messages and languages

The pattern of sand dunes in a desert forms structures that are easily recognizable from an aircraft. Carrying forward our information-based description of nature, could we say then that there exists a language of dunes? Sand carried by the wind "reads" the structures of existing dunes in a language consisting of ridges and gullies, and the structures we can see are the conservators capable of propagating their own information across time. Should we adopt this as a model rather than a purely physics-based analytical approach, exemplified by an equation to show the existence of periodic solutions for the height of the terrain?

Our answer is that an information-based model is a level of description that is to be used whenever it is considered to be useful. In the example of the dunes, this consisted of showing that some types of dune are better able than others to propagate what makes them different. These dunes were shown to be entities that come into being, live, interact with one another and die, acting under the effect of a code. Such a spatial code may generate a language, as one of the authors of this book has shown in the context of other types of landscape (Gaucherel *et al.* 2012). The information-based approach scores higher than a dynamic approach because of the fact that the state of the system depends on its past states over a longer period of time than is available in the dynamic approach. Now, as for what has been at work in the case of the dunes, the physicist may speak of sensitivity to initial conditions, while, for the mathematician, it may be non-ergodicity. If the current state of the system affects its future states, it would be reasonable to speak of information that is propagated across time, because of a code the system reads in order to determine its future.

A strict analysis of the information-based approach, however, presupposes a simplification, which is to identify a code, a message and a decoder. Here, a finer method would only see elementary interactions between individuals, between grains of sand, between molecules or between elementary particles. Each structure recognized by another structure is a message sent to the system's future. The message has a system-wide effect. It is this effect that constitutes the decoding. The decoding does not depend entirely on the environment (if it did, it would not have been decoding), but the environment influences it, whether by disturbing it or by directing it. This MDE schema that has been with us throughout our journey thus far constitutes for us a key to the reading of nature. What are the entities involved, what are their interactions, what are their invariants? And, above all, what is the information that is perpetuated? What code is used? What are its characteristics (analog, digital, combinatory, syntactic, etc.)? How has the message succeeded in surviving across time? These are not the only questions that arise before us about the organized aspect of nature.

While we cannot deny that information is experienced through physical media, it is necessary to resort to the domain of the abstract to obtain a definition of the concept in terms of messages and codes. We may speak of a sentence, forgetting that it grew out of populations of neurons. We may speak of a genetic sequence, forgetting that it is carried by a nucleic acid molecule. We may speak of the structure of a trophic network, forgetting that it is born from chance encounters between individuals of particular species. We may speak of a computer program without considering the machine on which it runs. Just as a book can give us much more than mere figures in black on a white background, nature gives us much more than a view of the structures it hosts.

5.7. The complexification of codes

Living nature today seems to us to be infinitely more complex than it must have been in the beginning of terrestrial time. Three billion years of evolution plus 600 or 700 million years of multicellular explorations have produced a breed of several million macroscopic species involved in intricate ecosystemic relationships. The human species likes to imagine itself at the pinnacle of this temporal ladder of complexity. Is it not itself creating complexity, by producing networks and machines that, someday, will compete with living nature?

Before we pursue this idea of complexification any further, we must clarify that we are not about to imply agreement with the prevailing myth of progress. Complexification is a possibility, not a necessity. If nature were to work so as to maximize complexity, then that does not say much for its efficiency. A key idea of Stephen Jay Gould was to show that macroevolution, which governs the fate of species over the long term, is not a directed process. Species have neither inertia nor momentum to push them on in the direction they have followed up until now. Viewed thus, the idea of progress is just a myth, and nothing more.

However, two phenomena may come to the rescue of the idea of complexification. The first is the one mentioned by Gould, namely the fact that the scale of complexity is open on the side of growth, but closed on the side of reduction (Gould 1989). A too simple being cannot live. Conversely, we do not know the theoretical limit of the sophistication of a living entity. Nature, just by blindly exploring the realm of possibilities, is inevitably going to create more and more complex forms.

The second idea is linked to the *ratchet effect*: certain complex forms or parts, once brought into being, strive to perpetuate themselves. For example, the eye, once evolved, remains active, except in the case of species that no longer need to use that organ. Complex forms serve as base camps for the exploration of more complex shapes.

Do these ideas of complexification apply to the codes of the living entity? Are nature's languages evolving toward greater sophistication? Is the information handled by nature constantly growing? What are the great landmarks of complexification in the history of the living entity? John Maynard Smith and Eörs Szathmáry published an inventory of some of these landmarks (Maynard Smith and Szathmáry 1995). There is the appearance of the first SSS, as far as we can describe it, in the prebiotic soup or in the physicochemical world that preceded it. There is also the appearance of multicellularity. That event occurred a little over 500 million years ago, perhaps soon after the earth-snowball event that had seen the planet ice-bound (except on an equatorial belt). The emergence of sociality, another major event, began with the phenomenon of coordinated movements, much like those that characterize schools of fish. Maynard Smith and Szathmáry see in the appearance of human language and in the resulting new form of social organization a case of a major transition in the living entity. From an anthropocentric point of view, they certainly appear to be right. The situation looks remarkable to us because it has seen the birth of our species. But is it "objectively" remarkable?

The great transitions that have been taking place in the living entity show a common characteristic, which is that they correspond to *emergent phenomena.* From a theoretical point of view, emergence may be defined on the basis of the complexity informing an aggregate (an aggregate of molecule, an aggregate of individuals, an aggregate of species or of any other entities). Since the aggregate entity is structured, there is emergence. From this point of view, and contrary to the popular adage, *the whole is less than the sum of its parts.* Collective behavior being made more predictable, sociality becomes a case of emergence, characterized by a base of complexity at the aggregate level.

Multicellularity is also an example of emergence (Maynard Smith and Szathmáry 1995). A cell divides, but, unlike what happens in the monocellular case, the copies remain together and the resulting aggregate adopts a coordinated behavior, much less complex than the behavior of the aggregate's components. The appearance of the first replicating molecule, while opening a window to the exploration of more and more complex replicating forms, is yet again a case of emergence. Instead of catalyzing or inhibiting a synthesis of other molecules of a predictable kind, the molecule is involved in a precise and unchanging cycle of reactions. The appearance of the replicating molecule is accompanied by the appearance of a structure of simplicity of the highest level, generating a cycle involving other structures.

Although they refer to the appearance of more complex individual forms that are also more difficult to outline, the major transitions that Maynard Smith and Szathmáry identified appear to us as emergent phenomena at a collective level and characterized by lower complexity. This is why we find them interesting. Owing to the latter feature, namely their lower complexity, emergent phenomena correspond to an increase in information in the living entity because, as we have seen in Chapter 4, information results from lowered complexity.

5.8. Complexification of languages

Nature evolving in the direction of increasing complexity appears to be a process that advances by steps, each step characterized by emergence, and each act of emergence characterized by a lowering of complexity. We note that at each step nature produces increasingly complex shapes, while the aggregate of these shapes is much less complex than would be the case if the complexity of each separate step were added together. This fact makes nature intelligible. One might, of course, retort that what we have called steps or major transitions are in fact cases in which a structure of a higher order appeared, and we perceived them as an emergence and as a simplification. That is probably true, because the scientist's eye introduces a considerable bias into this way of trying to globally describe nature.

However, one argument allows us to establish the view of a discrete succession of great transitions.

The living being is *built*. It possesses moreover the property of *autopoiesis*, that is, it builds itself (Varela *et al*. 1974). This fact has consequences for its complexity, for an obvious reason: a simple machine cannot generate complexity. Recall (Chapter 4) that we use the word "complex" in its technical sense, which is difficult to summarize or outline. It is easy to understand why the living being made its appearance as a simple being.

To push the argument to its limit, we may wonder how the living being succeeded in complexifying itself. The answer would be that it used another "machine" that, according to the definition, is much more complex than itself. It goes without saying that the living being is constituted of material substances, and uses the noise of its material environment as a source of complexity: from the point of view of information, the random has by definition the maximum complexity. This is yet another role of the environment in the MDE schema, the role of disruptor. The living entity, however, causes chance in random and minute controlled doses to take place in the fluctuations or copying errors (mutations). The living entity does this with extraordinary parsimony, because any excess would lead to impairment of autopoiesis or, in other words, to extinction.

We can see that the slow, fumbling progression of the living entity toward the complex was not just an illusion linked to our way of seeing it. Self-construction can only proceed step by step, utilizing the ratchet-like, forward-only movement available to it. Multicellularity is an example. The coordination of cells that share the same genetic information to form a coordinated collection defines a new "language". Once activated, this language begins to enjoy the advantages of stabilization and replication that give it perpetuity. We see here the ratchet effect, much like what we had seen in the case of the eye.

This extreme standpoint leads us to ask whether the codes of life are subject to selection, like the phenotype in the case of a living species. Behind multicellularity, as well as behind the organization of the eukaryotic nucleus cytoplasm, and behind sociality, we can see a *change of code* that has the effect of ensuring cohesion in the emerging structure. The code constitutes the real innovation that characterizes the emergent level, subject to selection.

By extension, ecosystemic codes seem to be their "phenotype", based on which nature carries out a sorting process in deciding on their viability. We might therefore expect that ecosystemic codes evolve, and they also spontaneously explore the range of possibilities from the simple to the complex.

While going through its genetic code, nature apparently examined several varieties of languages ranging from ecosystemic codes to systems of communication among humans and animals. These languages resemble one another in some ways while differing among themselves with regard to properties: they are either analog or digital, referent or non-referent, combinatory or holistic, arbitrary or iconic, syntactic or non-syntactic. Human language alone has the property of central recursion (Figure 5.1). The logical relations that exist among the properties (Chapter 1) may give indications of the history of these languages. While not all of the languages of nature are in a filial relationship, some could be, and it will be exciting to find out more about the subject. It would, for instance, be a fascinating exercise to model the non-arbitrary and non-combinatory precursors of the genetic code. The notion that human language appears to be the most complex of all known codes is perhaps just an illusion that has grown out of the fact that we have yet to understand all the languages of nature. However, under compulsion to explore the realm of possibilities in the domain of codes, nature apparently produced a species that specializes in information (Dessalles 2007b). Its language is unique because of these properties: it is digital, referent, compositional, arbitrary and syntactic all at the same time. Could this then signal the beginning of an accelerated flight forward that might see the arrival of increasingly complex codes?

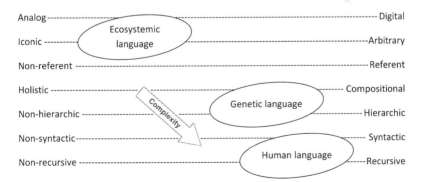

Figure 5.1. *A representation of the complexification of languages*

5.9. The re-creation of life

Human language finds a special place in the inventory of the major transitions in the history of life that Maynard Smith and Szathmáry (1995) identified. According to these authors, of the millions of animal species, of some 5,000 mammalian species, there is one particular species, ours, that has produced a communication code that constitutes one of the eight major transitions of the living being. What could be stranger than an observer who finds himself at the highest point of what he is called upon to describe objectively? Even so, we must take note of some facts that make our incursion into the realm of the living entity anything but trivial. The most outstanding of these facts is that we are probably about to bring into being what may conveniently be called the "sixth great extinction", an ecological disaster that may lead to a disappearance within just a few centuries (a mere instant on the scale of life) of some 80% of multicellular forms (Kolbert 2014). Aside from inflicting this devastating blight on the global ecosystem, and possibly setting off a long chain of catastrophes, how could we consider the emergence of our species to be a major transition in the living entity?

The human being has been evolving in order to become an information specialist (Chapter 1). We are now able to identify an entire collection of structures by simply observing a single aspect of the world that may appear to us unusually ordered or, more generally, unusually simple. If some structures in the living entity, such as genetic code, appeared slow in taking shape before us, it was so quite simply because we did not possess the technical and conceptual tools that now allow us to understand them. Other structures still remain hidden from our view, among them the codes that govern the generation of forms of multicellular beings. However, our knowledge of the structures of the living being is sufficiently advanced to enable us to disrupt its autopoiesis. Our understanding of the languages of nature is sufficiently fine grained to enable us to express ourselves using their codes. We can now create wholly synthetic chromosomes, and make them functional within cells. It cannot be denied, at the same time, that such an achievement is at the present time confined to the simplest chromosomes and cells that host similar chromosomes. However, we can already envisage the possibility of designing and building new codes of the living entity. That is the goal of synthetic biology.

As the human being is an element of the living entity, we might say that the living entity has discovered a new form of autopoiesis: through our agency, the living being can produce itself, not only through a multitude of short cycles associated with replicators, but also using a directed process. Like the hand in Gustav Escher's famous picture that draws itself, the living being has succeeded to a point where it can re-design itself. As in the case of all other transitions, the factor behind the innovation that allows us to shape life remains coincidental. If we are information specialists, it is because of reasons internal to our species (see Chapter 1) that have nothing to do with the future of the biosphere. This ability, it must be said, has allowed us to "read" crucial aspects of nature's working. Perhaps for good or ill, we are also learning to "write" in the living entity. We still do not know where this process will lead our species, the ecosystems that sustain us and even the biosphere itself.

The action of the human being on Earth has not stopped at the reshaping of life. We spoke in Chapter 1 of cultural memes, ideas that travel from one brain to another, and possess properties for efficient self-propagation. Human culture in this set appears to perpetuate itself and to evolve, if only bit by bit, through offspring after modification. Our computers, for instance, are not born of anything else. The earliest were designed in the mid-1900s on the model of the "analytical engine" that Charles Babbage had attempted to build in the closing years of the previous century himself inspired by the punched cards that Joseph Marie Jacquard had developed for his looms.

Some say that the track gauge (distance between the two rails of a pair) of Western railway systems has been copied from the span of stagecoaches (Blute 2010), the designers relying on the same kind of tools and the same sort of templates. The wheels of the ancient horse-drawn coaches had to pass through the tracks left in the ground by those that had preceded them, with some of them dating all the way back to the Roman times for the chariots of Roman nobles. In that sense, high-speed trains may well have blood ties to the war chariots of Julius Caesar! The universe of cultural artifacts may be described as a biocoenosis, with its own cycle of birth, reproduction and death, and above all its selection of forms that are able to endure. We may equally well describe this universe using codes and terms of information, something that Richard Dawkins did when he introduced the notion of meme (Dawkins 1976). We may then say that each human generation "reads" the artifactual language that offers it the culture in which it grew up, and it decodes and reproduces that language by modifying it.

5.10. And what about tomorrow?

Most of our artifacts, which may have a history behind them, may not necessarily have a future. However, there are some that have left their mark, or that will leave their mark, on the information-oriented history of humankind. What comes readily to mind in this context is the invention of writing, of numbers, of printing and of radio broadcasting that enabled the storing of information and its dissemination from one to many. Among recently invented artifacts, there are two that may mark a giant leap in the evolution of information on Earth. The first is the computer. This machine has not only expanded our capacity to handle existing information, but has also begun to create information on its own. At the present time, both kinds of information are perfectly intelligible to anyone ready to take the time to analyze them. In the foreseeable future, computers will be able to exchange information among themselves, while it remains qualitatively inaccessible to us, and in languages too complex for the human brain to understand. We are not there yet.

The other artifact that will leave its mark on history is already present among us: the World Wide Web, or, more familiarly, the Web. Information is alive on the Web: it is stored there, and copied and transmitted. The search engines that populate the Web space may trick us into overlooking the fact that informational entities have a material existence in some part of the hard drive. This *infosphere*, which no particular individual is known to have invented, seems to be developing all on its own. Its emergent working is seen to be increasingly rich and increasingly decoupled from the reality which gave it birth. It becomes more and more difficult to distinguish genuine information from fake information. However, we have to learn to survive in this informational jungle. The infosphere, an emanation from the biosphere, of which we are a part, may appear as a major transition of the living entity, as a new element in interaction with the biotope and the biocoenosis. It might happen, for example, that information that will prevail in the infosphere will influence the future climate of the planet or the human genome. Let us hope that this reason will play a role in the selection of such information entities.

We can view the world around us as being populated by things such as endless successions of new theatre events, a network of interactions or a scene in which everything is changing. We proposed in this book a view of the world from quite an unusual standpoint, as a system made up of codes and messages. These messages are addressed to the future of that world. Some of the entities are able to read an aspect of the state of the world, and change that aspect. We took our examples from human language, animal communication, genetics and ecosystems. It was possible in each case to explain why each informational analysis has interesting points to it. It is information that endures, well beyond the material substrate in which it is embedded. Information can only exist if it is read and decoded. The language allowing this to happen is not always the same. A trophic code does not resemble the genetic code, which, again, does not resemble a human language. Our analysis suggests a chronology in the properties of these languages that may become complex in the same way as the systems that host them. We have also listed the small number of principles underlying the large variety of natural languages, and which bring unity to nature, now being seen as an aggregate of information flows. We believe that this fresh approach will help produce new ideas and discoveries.

References

Allen, T.F.H. and Starr, T.B. (1982). *Hierarchy: Perspectives for Ecological Complexity*. University Chicago Press, Chicago.

Arenas, M. and Posada, D. (2014). Simulation of genome-wide evolution under heterogeneous substitution models and complex multispecies coalescent histories. *Mol. Biol. Evol.*, 31, 1295–1301.

Baum, D.A., Futuyma, D.J., Hoekstra, H.E., Lenski, R.E., Moore, A.J., Peichel, C.L., Schluter, D., and Whitlo, M.C. (2014). *The Princeton Guide to Evolution*. Princeton University Press, Princeton, New Jersey, USA.

Bennett, C.H. (1988). Logical depth and physical complexity. In *The Universal Turing Machine: A Half-Century Survey*, Herken, T. (ed.), Oxford University Press, Oxford, England, 227–257.

Bickerton, D. (1990). *Language and Species*. The University of Chicago Press, Chicago.

Black, D.L. (2003). Mechanisms of alternative pre-messenger RNA splicing. *Annu. Rev. Biochem.*, 72, 291–336.

Blute, M. (2010). *Darwinian Sociocultural Evolution*. Cambridge University Press, Cambridge, UK.

Brenner, S., Stretton, A.O.W., and Kaplan, S. (1965). Genetic code: The 'nonsense' triplets for chain termination and their suppression. *Nature*, 206, 994–998.

Capecchi, M.R. (1967). Polypeptide chain termination in vitro: Isolation of a release factor. *Proc. Natl. Acad. Sci. USA*, 58, 1144–1151.

Cheney, D.L. and Seyfarth, R.M. (1990). *How Monkeys See the World: Inside the Mind of Another Species*. University of Chicago Press, Chicago.

Danchin, É., Charmantier, A., Champagne, F.A., Mesoudi, A., Pujol, B., and Blanchet, S. (2011a). Beyond DNA: Integrating inclusive inheritance into an extended theory of evolution. *Nat. Rev. Genet.*, 12, 475–486.

Danchin, É., Charmantier, A., Champagne, F.A., Mesoudi, A., Pujol, B., and Blanchet, S. (2011b). Beyond DNA: Integrating inclusive inheritance into an extended theory of evolution. *Nat. Rev.*, 12, 475–486.

Darwin, C. (1859). *On the Origin of Species by Means of Natural Selection, or the Preservation of Favoured Races in the Struggle for Life.* John Murray, London.

Dawkins, R. (1976). *The Selfish Gene.* Oxford University Press, Oxford, England.

Delahaye, J.-P. (1994). *Information, complexité et hasard.* Hermès, Paris.

Dessalles, J.-L. (2007a). Storing events to retell them (Commentary on Suddendorf and Corballis: 'The evolution of foresight'). *Behav. Brain Sci.*, 30, 321–322.

Dessalles, J.-L. (2007b). *Why We Talk. The Evolutionary Origins of Language.* Oxford University Press, Oxford, England.

Dessalles, J.-L. (2010). From metonymy to syntax in the communication of events. In *The Emergence of Protolanguage – Holophrasis vs Compositionality*, Arbib, M. A. and Bickerton, D. (eds). John Benjamins Publishing Comp, Amsterdam, The Netherlands, 51–65.

Dessalles, J.-L. (2013). Algorithmic simplicity and relevance. In *Algorithmic Probability and Friends – LNAI 7070*, Dowe, D.L. (ed.). Springer Verlag, Berlin.

Diamond, J. (1997). *Guns, Germs, and Steel: The Fates of Human Societies.* W.W.Norton and Company, New York, NY.

Doolittle, W.F. (2000). Uprooting the tree of life. *Sci. Am.*, 282, 90–95.

Dorri, F., Mendelowitz, L., and Bravo H.C. (2016). MethylFlow: Cell-specific methylation pattern reconstruction from high-throughput bisulfite-converted DNA sequencing. *Bioinformatics*, 32, 1618–1624.

Dunbar, R.I.M. (1996). *Grooming, Gossip, and the Evolution of Language.* Harvard University Press, Cambridge, MA.

Eberhard, M.J.W. (1976). Sociobiology. The new synthesis by Edward O. Wilson. *Q. Rev. Biol.*, 51, 89–92.

Evans, J.H. and Evans, T.E. (1970). Methylation of the deoxyribonucleic acid of Physarum polycephalum at various periods during the mitotic cycle. *J. Biol. Chem.*, 245, 6436–6441.

Fisher, R.A. (1915). The evolution of sexual preference. *Eugenic Rev.*, 7, 184–192.

Fisher, R.A. (1918). The correlation between relatives on the supposition of Mendelian inheritance. *Philos. Trans. R. Soc. Edinburgh*, 52, 399–433.

Forman, R.T.T. and Godron, M. (1981). Patches and structural components for a landscape ecology. *BioScience*, 31, 733–740.

Francis, R.C. (2011). *Epigenetics. How Environment Shapes Our Genes*. W. W. Norton & Company, New York City, New York, USA.

Frontier, S., Pichod-Viale, D., Lepêtre, A., Davoult, D., and Luczak, C. (2008). *Ecosystèmes. Structure, Fonctionnement, Evolution*, 4th ed. Dunod, Paris.

Galtung, J. and Ruge, M.H. (1965). The structure of foreign news. *J. Peace Res.* 2, 64–91.

Gardner, A. and Úbeda, F. (2017). The meaning of intragenomic conflict. *Nat. Ecol. Evol*, 1(12), 1807-1815.

Gaucherel, C. (2006). Influence of spatial structures on ecological applications of extremal principles. *Ecol. Model.*, 193, 531–542.

Gaucherel, C. (2007). Multiscale heterogeneity map and associated scaling profile for landscape analysis. *Landscape and Urban Planning*. 82, 95–102.

Gaucherel, C. (2011). Self-organization of patchy landscapes: hidden optimization of ecological processes. *Journal of Ecosystem & Ecography*, 1(2), 105. doi: 10.4172/2157-7625.1000105.

Gaucherel, C. (2014). Ecosystem complexity through the lens of logical depth: Capturing ecosystem individuality. *Biol. Theory*. 31(10), 733-740.

Gaucherel, C., Boudon, F., Houet, T., Castets, M., and Godin, C. (2012). Understanding patchy landscape dynamics: Towards a landscape language. PLoS ONE. 10.1371/journal.pone.0046064.

Gaucherel, C., Théro, H., Puiseux, A., and Bonhomme, V. (2017). Understand ecosystem regime shifts by modelling ecosystem development using Boolean networks. *Ecol. Complexity*, 31, 104–114.

Gell-Mann, M. 1994. *The Quark and the Jaguar: Adventures in the Simple and the Complex*. St. Martin's Griffin, New York, NY.

Glansdorff, P. and Prigogine, I. (1971). *Thermodynamic Theory of Structure, Stability and Fluctuations*. Wiley-Interscience, New York, USA.

Gliddon, C.J. and Gouyon, P.H. (1989). The units of selection. *Trends Ecol. Evol.*, 4, 204–208.

Golse, F. and Saint-Raymond, L. (2004). The Navier-Stokes limit of the Boltzmann equation for bounded collision kernels. *Inventiones Math.*, 155, 81–161.

Gould, S.J. (1989). *Wonderful Life: The Burgess Shale and the Nature of History.* W. W. Norton & Company, New York.

Gouyon, P.-H., Henry J.-P., and Arnould J. (1997). *Les avatars du gène: théorie néodarwinienne de l'évolution.* Belin, Paris.

Gouyon, P.H., Vichot, F., and Van Damme, J. (1991). Nuclear-cytoplasmic male-sterility: single point equilibria versus limit cycles. *Am. Nat.*, 137, 498–514.

Graner, F. and Glazier, J.A. (1992). Simulation of biological cell sorting using a two-dimensional extended Potts model. *Phys. Rev. Lett.*, 69, 2013–2016.

Griffiths, P.E. (2001). Genetic information: A metaphor in search of a theory. Philos. Sci. 68, 394–412.

Haegeman, B. and Loreau, M. (2008). Limitations of entropy maximization in ecology. *Oikos*, 117, 1700–1710.

Hajj, K.A. and Whitehead, K.A. (2017). Tools for translation: Non-viral materials for therapeutic mRNA delivery. *Nat. Rev. Mater.*, 2, 17056.

Hamilton, W.D. (1967). Extraordinary sex ratios. A sex-ratio theory for sex linkage and inbreeding has new implications in cytogenetics and entomology. *Science* 156, 477–488.

Hamilton, W.D. (2002). *Narrow Roads of Gene Land.* Oxford University Press, Oxford, England.

Hauser, M.D. (1996). *The Evolution of Communication.* MIT Press, Cambridge.

Hauser, M.D., Chomsky N., and Fitch W.T. (2002). The faculty of language: What is it, who has it, and how did it evolve? *Science*, 298, 1569.

Hein, J., Schierup, M.H., and Wiuf, C. (2005). *Gene Genealogies, Variation and Evolution – A Primer in Coalescent Theory.* Oxford University Press, Oxford, England.

Holland, J.H. (1975). *Adaptation in Natural and Artificial Systems.* The University of Michigan Press, Ann Arbor, MI.

Holling, C.S. (1973). Resilience and stability of ecological systems. *Annu. Rev. Ecol. Syst.* 4, 1–23.

Hollister, J.D., Greiner, S., Wang, W., Wang, J., Zhang, Y., Wong, G.K., Wright, S.I., and Johnson, M.T. (2015). Recurrent loss of sex is associated with accumulation of deleterious mutations in Oenothera. *Mol. Biol. Evol.* 32, 896–905.

Hubbell, S. (2001). *The Unified Neutral Theory of Biodiversity and Biogeography.* Princeton University Press, Princeton, NJ.

Ising, E. (1925). Beitrag zur Theorie des Ferromagnetismus. *Zeitschrift Fur Physik*, 31, 253–258.

Jablonka, E. and Lamb, M.J. (2005). *Evolution in Four Dimensions*. MIT Press, Cambridge, MA, USA.

Jacob, F. (1993). *The Logic of Life. A History of Heredity*. Princeton University Press, Princeton, NJ.

Job, C. and Eberwine J. (1912). Localization and translation of mRNA in dendrites and axons. *Nat. Rev. Neurosci.*, 2, 889–898.

Johannsen, W. (1911). The genotype conception of heredity. *Am. Nat.*, 45, 129–159.

Kauffman, S.A. (1969). Metabolic stability and epigenesis in randomly constructed genetic nets. *J. Theor. Biol.*, 22, 437–467.

Kimura, M. (1983). *The Neutral Theory of Molecular Evolution*. Cambridge University Press, Cambridge, UK.

Kirchner, W.H. and Towne, W.F. (1994). The sensory basis of the honeybee's dance language. *Sci. Am.*, 6, 52–59.

Kolbert, E. (2014). *The Sixth Extinction: An Unnatural History*. Henry Holt & Company, New York City, USA.

Krebs, J.R. and Dawkins, R. (1984). Animal signals: Mind-reading and manipulation. In *Behavioural Ecology – An Evolutionary Approach*, 2nd ed., Krebs, J.R. and Davies, N.B. (eds). Blackwell Scientific Publications, Hoboken, New Jersey, USA.

Kwak, H., Lee, C., Park, H., and Moon, S. (2010). What is Twitter, a social network or a news media? *Proceedings of the 19th International World Wide Web (WWW) Conference*, ACM, Raleigh, NC, 591—600.

Lehmann, J. and Libchaber, A. (2008). Degeneracy of the genetic code and stability of the base pair at the second position of the anticodon. *RNA*, 14, 1264–1269.

Letunic, I. and Bork, P. (2007). *Interactive Tree Of Life (iTOL): An Online Tool for Phylogenetic Tree Display and Annotation*. Oxford University Press, Cambridge.

Levin, S.A. (2007). Theoretical ecology: Principles and applications. *Science*, 316, 1699–1700.

Lindeman, R. (1942). The trophic-dynamic aspect of ecology. *Ecology*, 23, 199–418.

Lotka, A.J. (1925). *Elements of Physical Biology*, Re-edition. Dover Publications, New York.

Lou Jost, B. (2006). Entropy and diversity. *Oikos*, 113, 363–375.

Lovelock, J. (2000). *The Ages of Gaia: A Biography of Our Living Earth.* Oxford University Press, Oxford, England.

Lovelock, J.E. and Margulis, L. (1974). Atmospheric homeostasis by and for the biosphere: The Gaia hypothesis. *Tellus, Series A. Stockholm: Int. Meteorological Inst.* 26, 2–10.

MacArthur, R. (1955). Fluctuations of animal populations, and a measure of community stability. *Ecology*, 36, 533–536.

Mandelbrot, B.B. (1983). *The Fractal Geometry of Nature.* Freeman, New York.

Manicacci, D., Couvet, D., Belhassen, E., Gouyon, P.H., and Atlan, A. (1996). Founder effects and sex ratio in the gynodioecious Thymus vulgaris L. *Mol. Ecol.*, 28, 63–72.

Margalef, R. (1968). *Perspectives in Ecological Theory.* University of Chicago Press, Chicago.

Margulis, L. and Chapman, M.J. (2009). *Kingdoms & Domains an Illustrated Guide to the Phyla of Life on Earth.* Academic Press/Elsevier, Amsterdam, The Netherlands.

May, R.M. (1973). Qualitative stability in model ecosystems. *Ecology*, 54, 638–641.

Maynard Smith, J. and Szathmáry, E. (1995). *The Major Transitions in Evolution.* Oxford University Press, Oxford, England.

MEA. (2005). *Current State and Trends Assessment.* Island Press, Washington, DC.

MEA. (2005). *Ecosystems and Human Well-Being: Synthesis.* Island Press, Washington, DC.

Mereschkowsky, K. (1910). Theorie der zwei Plasmaarten als Grundlage der Symbiogenesis, einer neuen Lehre von der Ent-stehung der Organismen. *Biol. Centralbl.*, 30, 353–367.

Miyazawa, K., Kipkorir, T., Tittman, S., and Manuelidis, L. (2012). Continuous production of prions after infectious particles are eliminated: Implications for Alzheimer's disease. *PLoS ONE*, 7, e35471.

Myers, N., Mittermeier, R.A., Mittermeier, C.G., Da Fonseca, G.A.B., and Kent, J. (2000). Biodiversity hotspots for conservation priorities. *Nature*, 403, 853–858.

Odum, E.P. and Odum, H.T. (1971). *Fundamentals of Ecology*, 3rd ed. Saunders, Philadelphia, PA.

Parmesan, C., Ryrholm, N., Stefanescu, C., Hill, J.K., Thomas, C.D., Descimon, H., Huntley, B., Kaila, L., Kullberg, J., Tammaru, T., Tennent, W.J., Thomas, J.A. and Warren, M. (1999). Poleward shifts in geographical ranges of butterfly species associated with regional warming. *Nature*, 399, 579–583. doi: 10.1038/21181.

Pray, L.A. (2008). DNA replication and causes of mutation. *Nat. Educ.* 1, 214.

Prusiner, S.B. (1991). Molecular biology of prion diseases. *Science*, 252, 1515–1522.

Rana, A.K. and Ankri, S. (2016). Reviving the RNA world: An insight into the appearance of RNA methyltransferases. *Front. Genet.*, 7, 99.

Reynolds, V. (2005). *The Chimpanzees of the Budongo Forest*. Oxford University Press, Oxford, England.

Rothemund, P.W. (2006). Folding DNA to create nanoscale shapes and patterns. *Nature*, 440, 297–302.

Schneider, E.D. and Kay, J.J. (1994). Life as a manifestation of the second law of thermodynamics. *Math. Comput. Model.*, 19, 25–48.

Scolnick, E., Tompkins, R., Caskey, T., and Nirenberg, M. (1968). Release factors differing in specificity for terminator codons. *Proc. Natl. Acad. Sci. USA*, 61, 772.

Shannon, C.E. (1948). A mathematical theory of communication. *Bell Syst. Technical J.*, 27, 379–423, 623–656.

Shannon, C.E. and Weaver, W. (1949). *The Mathematical Theory of Communication*. The University of Illinois Press, Urbana, IL.

Sjölander, K. (2004). Phylogenomic inference of protein molecular function: Advances and challenges. *Bioinformatics*, 20, 170–179.

Solé, R.V. and Bascompte, J. (2006). *Self-Organization in Complex Ecosystems*. Princeton University Press, Princeton, NJ.

Suddendorf, T. and Corballis, M.C. (2007). The evolution of foresight: What is mental time travel, and is it unique to humans? *Behav. Brain Sci.*, 30, 299–313.

Tansley, A. (1935). The use and abuse of vegetational concepts and terms. *Ecology*, 16, 284–307.

Theobald, D.L. (2010). A formal test of the theory of universal common ancestry. *Nature*, 465, 219–222.

Tilman, D., Reich, P.B., and Knops, J.M.H. (2006). Biodiversity and ecosystem stability in a decade-long grassland experiment. *Nature*, 441, 629–632.

Tomasetti, C., Li, L., and Vogelstein, B. (2017). Stem cell divisions, somatic mutations, cancer etiology, and cancer prevention. *Science*, 355, 1330–1334.

Tournebize, R. and Gaucherel, C. (2017). Language: A fresh concept to integrate syntactic and semantic information in life sciences. *BioSystems 160*, 1–9.

Turner, M.G. and Gardner, R.H. (1991). *Quantitative Methods in Landscape Ecology*. Springer Verlag, New York.

Tuteja, N. and Tuteja, R. (2004). Unraveling DNA helicases. Motif, structure, mechanism and function. *Eur. J. Biochem*, 271, 1849–1863.

Ulanowicz, R.E. (2001). Information theory in ecology. *Comput. Chem.*, 25, 393–399.

Varela, F.G., Maturana, H.R., and Uribe, R. (1974). Autopoiesis: The organization of living systems, its characterization and a model. *Biosystems*, 5, 187–196.

Von Frisch, K. (1953). *The Dancing Bees: An Account of the Life and Senses of the Honey Bee*. Harvest Books, New York.

Watson, J.D., Baker, T.A., Bell, S.P., Gann, A., Levine, M., and Oosick, R. (2008). *Molecular Biology of the Gene*. Pearson/Benjamin Cummings, San Francisco.

Webb, C.O., Ackerly, D.D., McPeek, M.A., and Donoghue, M.J. (2002). Phylogenies and community ecology. *Annu. Rev. Ecol. Syst.*, 33, 475–505.

Weismann, A. (1868). *Über die Berechtigung der Darwin'schen Theorie: ein akademischer Vortrag, gehalten am 8. Juli 1868 in der Aula der Universität zu Freiburg im Breisgau*. Engelmann, Leipzig.

Weismann, A. (1887). Zur Frage nach der Vererbung erworbener Eigenschaften. *Biol. Zbl.*, 6, 33–48.

Woese, C. and Fox, G. (1977). Phylogenetic structure of the prokaryotic domain: The primary kingdoms. *Proc. Natl. Acad. Sci. USA*, 74, 5088–5090.

Woese, C.R., Kandler, O., and Wheelis, M.L. (1990). Towards a natural system of organisms: Proposal for the domains Archaea, Bacteria, and Eucarya. *Proc. Natl. Acad. Sci. USA*, 87, 4576–4579.

Xu, J. (2002). Estimating the spontaneous mutation rate of loss of sex in the human pathogenic fungus Cryptococcus neoformans. *Genetics*, 162, 1157–1167.

Zahavi, A. and Zahavi, A. (1997). *The Handicap Principle*. Oxford University Press, New York.

Zahler, A.M., Damgaard, C.K., Kjems, J., and Caputi, M. (2003). SC35 and heterogeneous nuclear ribonucleoprotein A/B proteins bind to a juxtaposed exonic splicing enhancer/exonic splicing silencer element to regulate HIV-1 tat exon 2 splicing. *J. Biol. Chem.*, 279, 10077–10084.

Zhang, Y., Baranov, P.V., Atkins, J.F., and Gladyshev, V.N. (2005). Pyrrolysine and selenocysteine use dissimilar decoding strategies. *The Journal of Biological Chemistry*, 280 20740-20751.

Zuberbühler, K. (2006). Alarm calls. in Brown, K., (ed). *Encyclopedia of language and linguistics*, 2nd ed. Elsevier, Oxford, 143–155.

Index

Other titles from

in

Information Systems, Web and Pervasive Computing

2018

ARDUIN Pierre-Emmanuel
Insider Threats
(Advances in Information Systems Set – Volume 10)

CARMÈS Maryse
Digital Organizations Manufacturing: Scripts, Performativity and
Semiopolitics
(Intellectual Technologies Set – Volume 5)

CARRÉ Dominique, VIDAL Geneviève
Hyperconnectivity: Economical, Social and Environmental Challenges
(Computing and Connected Society Set – Volume 3)

CHAMOUX Jean-Pierre
The Digital Era 1: Big Data Stakes

DOUAY Nicolas
Urban Planning in the Digital Age
(Intellectual Technologies Set – Volume 6)

FABRE Renaud, BENSOUSSAN Alain
The Digital Factory for Knowledge: Production and Validation of Scientific
Results

GAUDIN Thierry, LACROIX Dominique, MAUREL Marie-Christine, POMEROL Jean-Charles
Life Sciences, Information Sciences

GAYARD Laurent
Darknet: Geopolitics and Uses
(Computing and Connected Society Set – Volume 2)

IAFRATE Fernando
Artificial Intelligence and Big Data: The Birth of a New Intelligence
(Advances in Information Systems Set – Volume 8)

LE DEUFF Olivier
Digital Humanities: History and Development
(Intellectual Technologies Set – Volume 4)

MANDRAN Nadine
Traceable Human Experiment Design Research: Theoretical Model and Practical Guide
(Advances in Information Systems Set – Volume 9)

PIVERT Olivier
NoSQL Data Models: Trends and Challenges

ROCHET Claude
Smart Cities: Reality or Fiction

SAUVAGNARGUES Sophie
Decision-making in Crisis Situations: Research and Innovation for Optimal Training

SEDKAOUI Soraya
Data Analytics and Big Data

SZONIECKY Samuel
Ecosystems Knowledge: Modeling and Analysis Method for Information and Communication
(Digital Tools and Uses Set – Volume 6)

2017

BOUHAÏ Nasreddine, SALEH Imad
Internet of Things: Evolutions and Innovations
(Digital Tools and Uses Set – Volume 4)

DUONG Véronique
Baidu SEO: Challenges and Intricacies of Marketing in China

LESAS Anne-Marie, MIRANDA Serge
The Art and Science of NFC Programming
(Intellectual Technologies Set – Volume 3)

LIEM André
Prospective Ergonomics
(Human-Machine Interaction Set – Volume 4)

MARSAULT Xavier
Eco-generative Design for Early Stages of Architecture
(Architecture and Computer Science Set – Volume 1)

REYES-GARCIA Everardo
The Image-Interface: Graphical Supports for Visual Information
(Digital Tools and Uses Set – Volume 3)

REYES-GARCIA Everardo, BOUHAÏ Nasreddine
Designing Interactive Hypermedia Systems
(Digital Tools and Uses Set – Volume 2)

SAÏD Karim, BAHRI KORBI Fadia
Asymmetric Alliances and Information Systems:Issues and Prospects
(Advances in Information Systems Set – Volume 7)

SZONIECKY Samuel, BOUHAÏ Nasreddine
Collective Intelligence and Digital Archives: Towards Knowledge Ecosystems
(Digital Tools and Uses Set – Volume 1)

2016

BEN CHOUIKHA Mona
Organizational Design for Knowledge Management

BERTOLO David
Interactions on Digital Tablets in the Context of 3D Geometry Learning
(Human-Machine Interaction Set – Volume 2)

BOUVARD Patricia, SUZANNE Hervé
Collective Intelligence Development in Business

EL FALLAH SEGHROUCHNI Amal, ISHIKAWA Fuyuki, HÉRAULT Laurent,
TOKUDA Hideyuki
Enablers for Smart Cities

FABRE Renaud, in collaboration with MESSERSCHMIDT-MARIET Quentin,
HOLVOET Margot
New Challenges for Knowledge

GAUDIELLO Ilaria, ZIBETTI Elisabetta
Learning Robotics, with Robotics, by Robotics
(Human-Machine Interaction Set – Volume 3)

HENROTIN Joseph
The Art of War in the Network Age
(Intellectual Technologies Set – Volume 1)

KITAJIMA Munéo
Memory and Action Selection in Human–Machine Interaction
(Human–Machine Interaction Set – Volume 1)

LAGRAÑA Fernando
E-mail and Behavioral Changes: Uses and Misuses of Electronic
Communications

LEIGNEL Jean-Louis, UNGARO Thierry, STAAR Adrien
Digital Transformation
(Advances in Information Systems Set – Volume 6)

NOYER Jean-Max
Transformation of Collective Intelligences
(Intellectual Technologies Set – Volume 2)

VENTRE Daniel
Information Warfare – 2nd edition

VITALIS André
The Uncertain Digital Revolution
(Computing and Connected Society Set – Volume 1)

2015

ARDUIN Pierre-Emmanuel, GRUNDSTEIN Michel, ROSENTHAL-SABROUX Camille
Information and Knowledge System
(Advances in Information Systems Set – Volume 2)

BÉRANGER Jérôme
Medical Information Systems Ethics

BRONNER Gérald
Belief and Misbelief Asymmetry on the Internet

IAFRATE Fernando
From Big Data to Smart Data
(Advances in Information Systems Set – Volume 1)

KRICHEN Saoussen, BEN JOUIDA Sihem
Supply Chain Management and its Applications in Computer Science

NEGRE Elsa
Information and Recommender Systems
(Advances in Information Systems Set – Volume 4)

POMEROL Jean-Charles, EPELBOIN Yves, THOURY Claire
MOOCs

2012

BUCHER Bénédicte, LE BER Florence
Innovative Software Development in GIS

GAUSSIER Eric, YVON François
Textual Information Access

STOCKINGER Peter
Audiovisual Archives: Digital Text and Discourse Analysis

VENTRE Daniel
Cyber Conflict

2011

BANOS Arnaud, THÉVENIN Thomas
Geographical Information and Urban Transport Systems

DAUPHINÉ André
Fractal Geography

LEMBERGER Pirmin, MOREL Mederic
Managing Complexity of Information Systems

STOCKINGER Peter
Introduction to Audiovisual Archives

STOCKINGER Peter
Digital Audiovisual Archives

VENTRE Daniel
Cyberwar and Information Warfare

2010

BONNET Pierre
Enterprise Data Governance

BRUNET Roger
Sustainable Geography

CARREGA Pierre
Geographical Information and Climatology

CAUVIN Colette, ESCOBAR Francisco, SERRADJ Aziz
Thematic Cartography – 3-volume series
Thematic Cartography and Transformations – Volume 1
Cartography and the Impact of the Quantitative Revolution – Volume 2
New Approaches in Thematic Cartography – Volume 3

LANGLOIS Patrice
Simulation of Complex Systems in GIS

MATHIS Philippe
Graphs and Networks – 2nd edition

THERIAULT Marius, DES ROSIERS François
Modeling Urban Dynamics

2009

BONNET Pierre, DETAVERNIER Jean-Michel, VAUQUIER Dominique
Sustainable IT Architecture: the Progressive Way of Overhauling Information Systems with SOA

PAPY Fabrice
Information Science

RIVARD François, ABOU HARB Georges, MERET Philippe
The Transverse Information System

ROCHE Stéphane, CARON Claude
Organizational Facets of GIS

2008

BRUGNOT Gérard
Spatial Management of Risks

FINKE Gerd
Operations Research and Networks

GUERMOND Yves
Modeling Process in Geography

KANEVSKI Michael
Advanced Mapping of Environmental Data

MANOUVRIER Bernard, LAURENT Ménard
Application Integration: EAI, B2B, BPM and SOA

PAPY Fabrice
Digital Libraries

2007

DOBESCH Hartwig, DUMOLARD Pierre, DYRAS Izabela
Spatial Interpolation for Climate Data

SANDERS Lena
Models in Spatial Analysis

2006

CLIQUET Gérard
Geomarketing

CORNIOU Jean-Pierre
Looking Back and Going Forward in IT

DEVILLERS Rodolphe, JEANSOULIN Robert
Fundamentals of Spatial Data Quality

Printed and bound by CPI Group (UK) Ltd, Croydon, CR0 4YY